Wild
MINNESOTA

A Celebration of Our State's Natural Beauty

Text by Shawn Perich
Photography by Gary Alan Nelson

Voyageur Press

First published in 2005 by Voyageur Press, an imprint of MBI Publishing Company, Galtier Plaza, Suite 200, 380 Jackson Street, St. Paul, MN 55105-3885 USA

Edited by Danielle J. Ibister
Designed by Andrea Rud
Printed in China

05   06   07   08   09   5   4   3   2   1

Library of Congress Cataloging-in-Publication Data

Perich, Shawn.
  Wild Minnesota : a celebration of our state's natural beauty / text by Shawn Perich ; photography by Gary Alan Nelson.
      p. cm.
  Includes bibliographical references and index.
  ISBN-13: 978-0-89658-681-9 (hardcover)
  ISBN-10: 0-89658-681-2 (hardcover)
  1. Minnesota--Pictorial works. 2. Minnesota--History, Local--Pictorial works. 3. Minnesota--Description and travel. 4. Natural history--Minnesota. 5. Natural history--Minnesota--Pictorial works. 6. Natural areas--Minnesota--Pictorial works. I. Nelson, Gary Alan, 1959- II. Title.
  F607.P445 2005
  977.6'022'2--dc22

2005011661

MBI titles are also available at discounts in bulk quantity for industrial or sales-promotional use. For details write to Special Sales Manager at MBI Publishing Company, Galtier Plaza, Suite 200, 380 Jackson Street, St. Paul, MN 55101-3885 USA.

On page 1
Autumn arrives in the Baptism River valley near Lake Superior.

On page 2
The silky St. Louis River pours over beds of angled slate and greywacke at Jay Cooke State Park south of Duluth.

On page 3
Morning light highlights fog on the St. Louis River as it races toward Lake Superior.

On page 4
Fresh snow blankets a tamarack and spruce bog in the Solana State Forest east of Mille Lacs Lake.

On page 5
Windblown fox tracks skirt bulrushes on Ringo Lake in central Minnesota.

On page 6
The Mississippi River gains strength as it winds through Crow Wing State Park near Brainerd.

On page 7
In the Agassiz National Wildlife Refuge, blooming goldenrod marks the onset of autumn.

On page 8
A mixed hardwood forest at Banning State Park shows off a kaleidoscope of autumn colors.

On page 9
Aspen and birch trees adorn the banks of the Temperance River near the Lake Superior shore.

On the title page
The lower falls of the Baptism River tumble through Tettegouche State Park.

Inset on the title page
A windblown red pine clings to a cliff and is rewarded with a bird's eye view of Lake Superior.

DEDICATION

To Joe, may the wild endure.
—Shawn Perich

To Mom and Dad, for exposing me to the outdoors.
—Gary Alan Nelson

Mist rises around a lone island on Fenske Lake in the Superior National Forest.

ACKNOWLEDGMENTS

A few acknowledgments need to be made to those who have advised, encouraged or assisted me with this project. John and Dewey, for fresh fish as well as countless moments of inspiration and amusement on all of those Boundary Waters canoe trips. Shawn, for food, shelter, clothing, conversation, and knowledge about the Superior country. Thank you, John and Mary Ann, of Gustaf's Galleries in Lindstrom, for those working vacations on Vermilion Lake. Carmelita, your enduring encouragement and the time you spent managing two kids, a dog, and a house while I was away is greatly appreciated. Finally, this book would not have happened if not for people, past and present, who have dedicated their time and efforts toward preserving the multitude of wild places that I have visited over the years.

—Gary Alan Nelson

Contents

Introduction
HEADWATERS OF THE CONTINENT   17

Chapter 1
GREAT RIVERS   25

Chapter 2
THE NORTH SHORE   47

Chapter 3
LAND OF LAKES   69

Chapter 4
THE CANOE COUNTRY   87

Chapter 5

THE ENDURING PRAIRIE   107

Chapter 6

FOREST REALMS   127

Chapter 7

A PASSION FOR THE WILD: MINNESOTA'S CONSERVATION LEGACY   147

Appendix

CONSERVATION ORGANIZATIONS   157

INDEX   158

ABOUT THE AUTHOR AND PHOTOGRAPHER   160

HEADWATERS OF THE CONTINENT

Above
A common loon and its one-day-old
chick explore a Minnesota lake.
(Photograph © Bill Marchel)

Left
Sky-blue reflections highlight rapids on the
St. Louis River in Jay Cooke State Park.

When a thunderstorm passes across Minnesota, its rains become the lifeblood of the continent. The waters of the Mississippi River, the Great Lakes, and Hudson Bay drainages originate here, welling up in black spruce bogs and beaver ponds, tumbling through shady forest valleys, and pausing often to form a myriad of lakes. Eventually, the waters gather to become mighty rivers: the Red, the Rainy, the St. Louis, the St. Croix, the Minnesota, and the Mississippi. Waters originating in Minnesota eventually flow to the Arctic Ocean, the North Atlantic, and the Gulf of Mexico.

Although much of eastern North America lies downstream from Minnesota, travelers often remark that the state they see from major highways looks as flat as a pan. Blame it on the Ice Age. Glaciation leveled and scoured Minnesota's landscape as recently as twelve thousand years ago. The state's many lakes and marshes are remnants of massive, post-glacial lakes that formed when the mile-high walls of ice slowly receded. The Minnesota and the St. Croix rivers flow through deep valleys carved by churning glacial rivers that poured from the outlets of the ancient Lakes Agassiz and Duluth. Northwestern Minnesota was submerged beneath the southern lobe of 110,000-square-mile glacial Lake Agassiz. Its outlet, the glacial River Warren, followed the present-day course of the Minnesota River. Lake Superior is the remnant of glacial Lake Duluth. South of Mankato was glacial Lake Minnesota. Lakes Grantsburg, Aitkin, and Upham covered much of east-central and north-central Minnesota, in areas where today's landscape is defined by vast swamps and bogs. In the northern forest, rolling hills are glacial gravel deposits called moraines. Also deposited were glacial erratics, boulders of varied shapes and sizes that confound farmers and gardeners across the state. The only significant relief in Minnesota's topography occurs where the unyielding rock of the Canadian Shield resisted the ice in the northeast and the unglaciated bluff country, or Driftless Area, in the southeast.

The state's highest point—Eagle Mountain in the Sawtooth Range, near the tip of the northeastern Arrowhead—rises just 2,301 feet above sea level. The lowest point—Lake Superior, at 602 feet above sea level— is only a few miles away. The forested ridges of the North Shore may not match the Rockies, but they can test the mettle of seasoned hikers, as many have discovered along the Superior Hiking Trail. High points on the trail offer distant vistas of blue Superior, then long slopes drop down into cool, shaded valleys, where trout streams the color of strong tea tumble toward the lake. The North Shore's towering headlands impeded early travelers. The eight-mile Grand Portage was a well-trodden pathway during the Fur Trade Era. Voyageurs carried heavy packs filled with beaver skins and other trade goods from Lake Superior to Fort Charlotte alongside the lower reaches of the Pigeon River in order to avoid the rapids, waterfalls, and canyons on this stretch.

Above
Ghost surf washes over crimson pebbles on the North Shore.

Facing page
Lake Superior attempts to escape its boundaries near Lutsen.

Topography in southeastern Minnesota is dramatic, too. High bluffs rise above rivers like the Root and the Zumbro, which twist through scenic valleys en route to the Mississippi River. Unlike the North Shore's Sawtooths, which are the time-worn remains of ancient volcanic thrusts, southeast Minnesota's limestone bluffs were carved by erosion. The level farmland above the bluffs overlies a honeycomb of sinkholes, fissures, and caverns created by water seeping through the soft stone. The subterranean water re-emerges, clear and cold, from a myriad of springs that feed bluff-country trout creeks, trickles destined for the distant Gulf of Mexico.

By contrast, northwestern Minnesota is pancake-flat and wet, the boggy remnant of glacial Lake Agassiz. Low gravel ridges, formed by receding beaches on the ancient lake, provide the only hills in an otherwise level topography. Here, the water runs north to Hudson Bay in one major drainage. The Red River of the North originates in Lake Traverse and, fed by swampy peat bogs and shallow basins like Upper and Lower Red Lake, flows to Manitoba's Lake Winnipeg. The northwest landscape is a mix of aspen forest and prairie, most of which has been converted to agriculture. The Red River valley's exceptionally rich soil has made the area famous for its sugar-beet production. Farms are large and the countryside is lightly inhabited. Long views are the norm. While the Red River drainage lacks the tall pines and sparkling lakes that typify the north country, it boasts an abundance of wildlife, including the state's only elk herds. Agassiz and Tamarac National Wildlife Refuges, as well as numerous state wildlife management areas, attract clouds of migrating waterfowl, shorebirds, raptors, and songbirds every spring and fall, making these areas popular destinations for birders and hunters.

Head east from "the Valley," as locals call it, and you enter the lake country of north-central Minnesota. The Mississippi River rises here among low, rolling hills cloaked with pine and hardwood forests. Thousands of interconnected lakes—ranging from backwoods potholes to sprawling waters like Winnibigoshish, Bowstring, Cass, and Leech lakes—feed the coursing river. With the natural world near at hand, the lake country's warm summers and snowy winters provide excellent opportunities for recreation and relaxing. This is cabin country, where a fishing boat is parked in every driveway and the opening day of deer season is an unofficial holiday. In the summer, the population swells in Grand Rapids, Brainerd, Bemidji, and Walker, when everyone is "up at the lake." In the winter, ice-fishing shanties dot the frozen waters and snowmobiles zip along snowy trails.

Those who prefer quieter sports often head farther north, to the canoe country along the Canadian border. The Boundary Waters Canoe Area Wilderness is a nationally acclaimed wild area. Hundreds of unspoiled lakes sit like gems in a brooding boreal forest, accessible only by canoe. When winter arrives, campers undaunted by deep snows and bitterly cold nights venture into the wilderness on dog sled, ski, or snowshoe to enjoy winter's splendor in solitude. West of the Boundary Waters is Voyageurs National Park, where the interconnected waters of Rainy, Kabetogama, and Namakan lakes are a boating and angling paradise. Some park visitors "rough

Red pine trees, some over two hundred years old, make a stand in Preachers Grove at Itasca State Park.

it" on a rented houseboat, exploring the lakes by day and pulling up on the beach of a secluded, pine-studded island for the night.

It stretches the imagination to consider that the vastly different landscapes of the canoe country and the prairie occur in the same state. The prairie is open, a sea of grass, with islands of trees growing along waterways or in scattered oak groves called savannahs. Shallow lakes and extensive wetlands—called prairie potholes—provide productive habitat for a range of wildlife species, especially nesting and migrating waterfowl. Across southern and western Minnesota, just a remnant of the original prairie remains. These scattered tracts are ecological storehouses of native plants, butterflies, birds, and other species that once existed in great abundance. Some prairie species, like bison, are gone from the Minnesota prairie, although ancient, bleached bison bones still surface along exposed stream banks. The hand of man dominates today's agricultural landscape, but the spirit of the wild prairie endures.

A storm front drifts over Scott Lake and a stand of birch, aspen, spruce, and tamarack trees in Superior National Forest.

The clear water of the Root River flows to the Mississippi River.

The hand of man is less evident in the woods, though significant changes have occurred here, too. Minnesota's original forests were cut down to provide lumber for a growing nation, then ravaged by wild fires and cleared by settlers. Little of the forest primeval remains. Today, the remaining groves of tall pines exist mostly in protected areas such as Itasca State Park. The old-growth hardwood forests of south-central Minnesota's Big Woods are similarly limited to parks and preserves. Overall, however, Minnesota's forests have remained ecologically healthy and economically productive. From the bluff country's oak and hickory ridges to the north country's aspen and birch woods, forests provide important recreational resources and a sustainable source of wood products. Modern forestry practices help protect the environment, provide a continuous supply of wood fiber, and ensure that future generations of Minnesotans inherit the state's forest legacy.

Our inheritance of woodlands, grasslands, lakes, and wilderness did not occur by happenstance. Minnesota has a long and rich conservation history. The foresight of previous generations led to a statewide network of parks, forests, nature preserves, historic sites, and wildlife areas. Political battles were fought to establish and protect our crown jewels: the Boundary Waters and Voyageurs National Park. We have not only a wealth of wild places but also the means for the public to enjoy them. Outdoor recreation forms an integral part of our state identity. With millions of acres of public forests, thousands of lakes and streams, and hundreds of public parks and natural areas, no Minnesotan has to travel far to find an accessible wild place. A long-standing access program administered by the Minnesota Department of Natural Resources (DNR) has developed public launch sites on many lakes and streams. Thousands of miles of public trails for hiking, bicycling, snowmobiling, and cross-country skiing provide endless opportunities to enjoy the natural world. It is not surprising that Minnesotans are uncommonly committed to protecting and preserving the wild.

The conservation struggle continues. While we have made great strides in public land acquisition, fish and wildlife management, prairie restoration, and sustainable forestry, an expanding population challenges our ability to protect wild resources from new threats such as urban sprawl, lakeshore development, wetland drainage, water pollution, and recreational conflicts. A host of public agencies and private organizations work to address these and other environmental issues, but they often lack the funding, manpower, and political support necessary to get the job done. Instead of losing faith, the conservation movement grows stronger. Many Minnesotans volunteer their time to clubs and organizations devoted to the protection and conservation of fish and wildlife, parks, trails, natural areas, and the environment. Their efforts will ensure we pass on a wild Minnesota to those who will follow in our footsteps.

A change of season creates fresh foliage in the Richard Dorer Memorial Hardwood Forest in southeastern Minnesota.

Chapter 1

GREAT RIVERS

Above
The Pigeon River, forming the border between
Minnesota and Canada, drops 120 feet at Grand
Portage State Park, making it the highest
waterfall in the state.

Left
Marbled skies and autumn colors frame
Dragon's Tooth Rapids on the Kettle River
in Banning State Park.

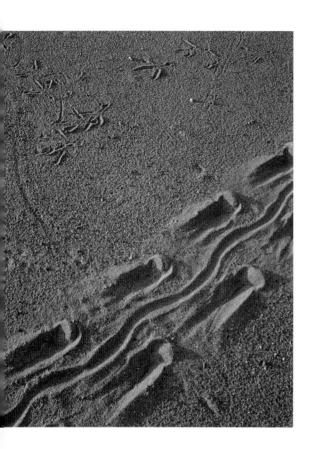

Snapping turtle and great blue heron tracks mark a sandbar in the Upper Mississippi.

Every summer at Itasca State Park, thousands of people step across the Mississippi River. At the outlet of Lake Itasca, where the river officially begins, they walk on stepping stones placed there by young men who worked for the Civilian Conservation Corps during the Great Depression. The Mississippi is Minnesota's natal coil, a waterway born amid pine-clad hills and nourished with the waters of lakes large and small. The river's upper reaches in north-central Minnesota flow through sweeping wild rice stands and windswept walleye lakes. By the time it reaches central Minnesota, passing Little Falls and St. Cloud, the young river runs strong and sure, flowing quick and clean over cobble and boulders. At Minneapolis, the river growls over what remains of St. Anthony Falls, the upstream limit of navigation. Below St. Paul, the river widens, losing itself in a labyrinth of backwaters and side channels. Here, locks and dams harness the river, and the main channel is dredged to provide a route for commercial barges and other watercraft.

Though his hometown of Hannibal, Missouri, lies hundreds of miles downstream, this is the Mississippi of Mark Twain. On summer days, you might see a paddle-wheel steamer churning up the channel or docked at the wharf in Wabasha or another river town. Slip a canoe into a Houston County backwater and you enter the world of Huckleberry Finn. The mosaic of islands and marshes remains wild, though dams and dredging have stilled the currents that flowed through the serpentine channels in Huck's day. The backwaters still flood when the river runs high in spring and early summer, refreshing the aquatic ecosystem but also, unfortunately, delivering a fresh deposit of silt—the eroded topsoil washed away from distant farmlands. Siltation confounds conservation efforts, because it fills in backwater pools and smothers native vegetation, especially where dams disrupt natural currents.

Though the river ecosystem has changed since Twain's era, it remains unique. Unusual fish species swim in the backwaters, including gar, buffalo fish, and bowfin, as well as the more common bluegill and largemouth bass. Several turtle species, including the rare Blandings turtle, live in the sloughs and build nests in the adjacent sand dunes. "Southern" wildlife species, such as wild turkey and opossum, populate the bottomland islands. The Mississippi River valley serves as a continental bird migration corridor. In the fall, large flocks of canvasback ducks and tundra swans congregate on pools along the river. Wintering eagles at Wabasha attract thousands of birders annually.

Several bluff country rivers feed the Mississippi. The Cannon, Zumbro, Whitewater, and Root rivers originate on the southeast's prairie uplands and carve beautiful, forested valleys as they gather the flows of spring-fed tributary creeks. Sculpting the landscape, the rivers define the character of the southeast. Tidy farms and quaint villages, pastoral remnants of an earlier, rural era, make the bluff country seem to be a land that time forgot, a sensation reinforced when you encounter an Amish horse and buggy along a twisting backroad. But this beautiful place can more

An erratic sandbar in the Upper Mississippi National Wildlife Refuge, in the southeastern part of the state, increases or diminishes in size depending on the flow of the river.

aptly be described as the land that time has healed. Today's forests and farms cover the scars of past land abuse.

Early settlers found a paradise in the bluff country. Running swift and free, the Mississippi teamed with fish, waterfowl, furbearers, and game. Shaded by ancient hardwoods, the cold, clear tributary rivers and creeks swarmed with native brook trout. In the fall, the piercing bugles of rutting elk echoed through the hills. Bison grazed on bluff-top prairies. For the settlers, this natural bounty provided the resources to build communities—and a nation. They cut down the mighty hardwoods to make lumber, cleared forests, and broke the prairie sod to plant crops.

As settlement expanded, so did land clearing. The settlers cut down the trees on steep hillsides, which led to ecological disaster. Whenever it rained, soil on the slopes washed downhill. Erosion occurred on a scale difficult to imagine today. Flash flooding was a recurring problem, and the raging waters destroyed farms and buried buildings beneath tons of silt. The once-clear trout streams became muddy ditches, their banks torn and ragged from erosion. Paradise was lost.

The collapse of farming in the valleys eventually brought about changes. Reforestation programs in the mid-twentieth century stabilized slopes and curbed

Wolf Creek tumbles over a ledge on its way to the Kettle River in Banning State Park.

erosion. As the streams cleared, they were stocked with trout—primarily brown trout, a widely introduced European species that is more tolerant of warmer water temperatures and more wary of humans than native brookies. White-tailed deer repopulated the new forests. In the latter half of the twentieth century, wildlife biologists introduced wild turkeys to the southeast. It is thought the big birds may have been native to bluff country, although the area would have represented the northernmost extent of their range. Today, wild turkeys thrive in the bluff country, where they are commonly seen in fields and alongside roads. Go out early on a soft spring morning and you can listen to them gobbling to greet the dawn. For many folks, it is a sound that has come to symbolize the bluff country's wild side.

Further north, in tall white pines along the St. Croix Wild and Scenic Riverway, the bald eagle is a wild emblem. The St. Croix, which rises in northwestern Wisconsin, is a classic northern river, tumbling with rapids and foam-flecked pools, as are its Minnesota tributaries, the Kettle and Snake rivers. Protected from development by its federal Wild and Scenic designations, along with a wealth of public lands along its banks, the St. Croix is a paddler's paradise.

In some respects, its official Wild status belies the river's industrial past. Minnesota's first European settlers made their homes along the St. Croix at Stillwater. Fortunes were made along the river. During the 1800s, workers harvested the vast pineries of the St. Croix drainage, floating the mighty logs downstream to sawmills in Stillwater and other river communities. The lumbering era didn't last long; the seemingly endless stands of pine were soon cut down. Scattered pines, aged concrete dams, and dilapidated rockworks remain, among the only present-day reminders of the logging era. Along forested ridges, now dominated by aspen, maple, and other hardwoods, you may encounter huge, charred stumps, remnants of an ancient forest that disappeared more than a century ago.

The St. Croix is a popular recreational river. The upper reaches, crossed by few roads, are best explored by canoe. Stony riffles and rapids alternate with deep, sandy pools. Smallmouth bass lurk among the rocks and beneath overhanging debris, muskies lie in ambush along quiet eddies, and walleyes patrol deeper currents. The river supports a self-sustaining lake sturgeon population. An angler caught the state record, weighing an amazing 94 pounds 4 ounces, in the tributary Kettle River in 1994. Deer, wild turkey, and—further north—gray wolves roam the St. Croix watershed. Large tracts of public land, including the St. Croix Wild River and William O'Brien state parks, and the Chengwatana and St. Croix state forests, provide ample wildlife habitat, as well as opportunities for hiking and cross-country skiing.

River scenery is outstanding. The St. Croix follows the bed of a post-glacial river that flowed out of Lake Minong, the mighty predecessor of Lake Superior. Powerful currents, laden with silt and debris, cut a chasm through sedimentary rock. The Dalles of the St. Croix, downstream from Taylors Falls, contains sculpted rock formations most easily viewed from the water. Along the riverside hiking trail at Interstate State Park, you can find depressions in the soft bedrock called kettles, created thousands of years ago by the abrasive action of small stones in swirling glacial currents. Below the Dalles, the river widens and valley forests grow more lush—southerly influences of the approaching Mississippi River. The great rivers join at the city of Hastings, creating a mile-wide flow.

Upstream from Hastings, the state's largest western tributary, the muddy Minnesota River, enters the Mississippi. While the St. Croix and the upper Mississippi are born in the north woods, the Minnesota River is a child of the prairie. Big Stone Lake on the South Dakota border forms its headwaters. The Minnesota's upper

Fog-shrouded white pines tower over the St. Croix National Scenic River on the border between Minnesota and Wisconsin.

reaches pass through the wild lands of Big Stone National Wildlife Refuge, the Lac qui Parle Wildlife Management Area, two state parks, and a number of prairie preserves. Combined, these areas represent the most extensive grasslands in western Minnesota. Prairie wildlife abounds here. In spring and fall, migrating waterfowl stop at the lakes and marshes flanking the upper Minnesota River. Lac qui Parle is especially famed for its Canada geese, which rest here in the fall en route from nesting grounds in Manitoba and Saskatchewan. Lac qui Parle forms part of an international series of refuges that allow geese to rest undisturbed during their migrations.

Not so many years ago, Lac qui Parle represented one of a handful of locations in Minnesota where you could see large numbers of Canada geese. In recent decades, the big birds have become so common throughout the state that some residents take them for granted or even consider them a nuisance. Few folks know that Minnesota successfully restored its resident Canada geese from the brink of extinction.

Canada geese vary in size, ranging from three to fifteen pounds. When European settlers arrived on the prairie, they found especially large Canadas—weighing twelve pounds or more—nesting on lakes and potholes. Subsistence and market hunting wiped them out by the early 1900s. In fact, biologists long believed the "giant" Canada geese a myth. Then, in the early 1960s, a captive flock of giant Canadas, descendants of wild birds, was discovered in Rochester. The state stocked birds originating from this flock in likely nesting locations in Minnesota and elsewhere. Suburban and agricultural landscapes proved to be excellent, predator-free habitat, with ponds for nesting and lawns for grazing. The geese prospered and, by the early 1990s, had firmly established themselves in nearly all the suitable habitat in the state, including parks, golf courses, and backyards throughout the Twin Cities metropolitan area.

The broad, wooded valley of the Minnesota River serves as a corridor for other wildlife species as well. Wild turkeys have spread from stocking sites to virtually all woodlands along the river and its tributaries. White-tailed deer, once uncommon throughout southern and western Minnesota, now live in abundance in the valley, perhaps attracting visits from a roving, rarely seen predator. In recent years, residents have reported cougar sightings along the river corridor. In 2002, police officers shot and killed a cougar in a suburban park near Minneapolis. Biologists are unsure of the origins of the wild cats. Some believe they were released from captivity, but it is plausible that Minnesota supports a small number of wild wanderers. The nearest established cougar populations live in the Black Hills of South Dakota. Perhaps young cougars seeking to establish their own territory roam eastward as far as the Minnesota River valley.

The river historically served as a travel corridor for humans, too. European traders and trappers—and, later, settlers—followed the river westward across the state. Minnesota river towns account for the state's oldest settlements: The south-

Both photos
Lichen-covered bedrock lines the banks of the Kettle River in the east-central part of the state. A ten-mile stretch of the Kettle River is designated a state Wild and Scenic River.

central city of St. Peter was initially the state capital. Pioneer farmers displaced the valley's original occupants, the Lakota. Simmering tension between the settlers and Lakota boiled over in the late summer of 1862, when American Indian bands throughout the valley joined a general uprising. Several hundred settlers and American Indians were killed before U.S. troops suppressed the uprising. Of the Lakota, 309 were sentenced to hang; President Abraham Lincoln pardoned all but 38. Their hanging remains the largest mass execution in U.S. history. The tragic story of the uprising is told at Fort Ridgely State Park. Several historic sites commemorate battles and events associated with the short war.

Along the Minnesota River, the Wild West has given way to contemporary country. Tidy farms with endless rows of corn and soybeans dominate the landscape. In recent years, focused farmland conservation subsidies have been used to plant filter strips of permanent vegetation along waterways, restore wetlands, and combat soil erosion throughout the watershed. River towns are investing in wastewater treatment upgrades that will help clean up the river, too. The Mississippi River's sediment-laden outflow in the Gulf of Mexico creates a vast, oxygen-depleted "dead zone." Since the Minnesota River counts among the most polluted waters in the Mississippi River drainage, conservationists hope water-quality improvements eventually will be measurable in the gulf. Two centuries of recorded history attest to a river famous for periodic spring floods. Flooding occurs naturally, though many scientists believe ditching and wetland drainage throughout the watershed accelerate runoff and contribute to flood severity. High water damages and disrupts communities up and down the river. The receding flood deposits silt and debris along the banks and bottoms. And the river, changed but the same, rolls on.

Big rivers support big fish, and unusual ones at that. Consider the paddlefish, an ancient species found only in large rivers such as the lower St. Croix and the Mississippi below St. Paul's Ford Dam. The fish's long, paddle-like snout bears special sensors that detect minute electrical currents generated by plankton, the tiny plants and animals it eats. Plankton make for a surprisingly nutritious food source, and paddlefish grow rapidly, reaching weights of thirty to fifty pounds. Once abundant, paddlefish have declined as dams and pollution have adversely affected their habitat. Another monster of river depths, the flathead catfish, may top fifty pounds. Common in big rivers, flatheads lurk in deep pools and backwaters, where they prey on other fish. Bigger still is the lake sturgeon, which may surpass six feet in length. Other leviathans of the currents include bigmouth buffalo fish, common carp, and northern pike, all of which may achieve weights of thirty pounds or more.

Commercial fishing once served as an economic mainstay for river communities and still occurs in some locales. A parallel industry formed around the collection of freshwater mussels. The colorful names of native mussels—the purple wartyback, plain mucket, pink heel-splitter, elktoe, and snuffbox—conjure images of our pioneer past. Before European settlers, native people had harvested mussels for thousands of years. Commercial harvest began in the 1800s, first for pearls and later for

Both photos
A cannon points toward the barracks and officers' quarters at historic Fort Snelling in St. Paul. The sutler's store has been recreated to reflect the past.

mussel shells to make buttons. More recently, tiny nuggets of crushed mussel shell were implanted in live oysters to create pearls.

Mussels have an intriguing natural history. These bivalve mollusks have two hard shells, or valves, connected by a hinge. Inside the valves, a simple body is covered by tissue called a mantle. The mussel has a single foot that reaches out between the valves and slowly pulls the animal forward. To eat, a mussel siphons plankton and microscopic debris from the water. It has a mouth but no head or eyes.

Most interesting is the way mussels reproduce. Tiny larvae attach themselves to living fish and form cysts in their tissue. When a larva develops into a juvenile mussel—a process that, depending upon the species, takes weeks or months—the cyst breaks open and the mussel drops off. Mussels may live ten to forty years or more, and their valves form annual growth rings like trees. In a good habitat, large numbers of adult mussels form a "bed" on the river bottom.

Pollution, over-harvesting, and the damming of river systems have led to precipitous declines in mussel populations. Over half of Minnesota's forty-nine native mussel species are officially listed as endangered, threatened, or of special concern. Two species were extirpated from the state. The collection of live mussels is now illegal.

Biologists hope some native mussel populations will slowly recover, though the rapid spread of exotic zebra mussels in the Mississippi drainage poses a new threat. Simply put, the invasive zebra mussels reproduce so prolifically that they can carpet river-bottom habitat formerly used by native species.

While human activity has influenced—and degraded, to some extent—river ecosystems, the great river corridors remain surprisingly wild, even within the metropolitan area. Most of the Minnesota River within the metro region is contained in the Minnesota Valley National Fish and Wildlife Refuge, though only the most ardent outdoor enthusiasts make use of this little-known resource. Visitors to Fort Snelling State Park, located along the Minnesota River beneath the flight path of nearby Minneapolis-St. Paul International Airport, come primarily to see the historic site for which it is named. But the park has a wild side, too. Aside from the occasional roar of a jet passing overhead, the park offers a great escape to urban dwellers looking for a close-to-home place to get away from it all. Secluded, sandy beaches along the river offer solitude in the midst of the city. The densely wooded river bottoms support a large population of white-tailed deer and provide habitat for an array of wildlife species, including great blue herons, wood ducks, and beavers.

You might say a muddy old river isn't much of a place to spend a day, but a river rat from New Ulm or Winona would surely disagree. Once you push off shore in a flat-bottomed jon boat, all that really matters is the river. You can spend years learning its moods and rhythms. From flood to drought, blizzard to heat wave, a great river is a study of natural extremes. A flooded marsh where pike spawn in April

may be a dry meadow in August. The turtles of July bask on shoreline logs that lay buried beneath windswept snow drifts in January. Within this harsh juxtaposition, life flourishes.

The real attraction of a great river is the way it connects you to distant places. From the middle of Lake Pepin in the bluff country of southeastern Minnesota, St. Louis doesn't seem so far away, and even New Orleans is a possibility. Out on the river, we all become Huck Finn.

Aspen and birch trees make themselves apparent during autumn in the Cascade River valley.

An oak tree and lingering clouds frame a setting sun in the Minnesota Valley National Fish and Wildlife Refuge along the Minnesota River in the south-central part of the state.

Tussocks of grass pop out of a bog along the West Savanna River near McGregor, west of Duluth.

The gathered waters of the St. Louis River make a final crescendo along a narrow stretch in Jay Cooke State Park before entering the river estuary and, eventually, Lake Superior. The river fluctuates wildly in volume depending on runoff and rainfall.

Right
Wintering bald eagles draw birders to the Mississippi
River. (Photograph © Bill Marchel)

Below
The St. Louis River flows through
freshly fallen snow.

Left
Flowing water creates ice patterns on a small creek in
the St. Croix River valley.

Below
A spring-swollen Minneopa Creek cascades over a cliff
at Minneopa State Park near Mankato.

Above, top
Successful restoration efforts have allowed
Minnesota's native Canada geese to flourish.
(Photograph © Bill Marchel)

Above, bottom
Scattered bricks are all that remain
of most of the buildings at the historic Upper
Sioux, or Yellow Medicine, Indian Agency. The
agency was destroyed during the U.S.–Dakota
Conflict of 1862.

Left
Towering cliffs, referred to as the Dalles, provide
a splendid view of the St. Croix National Scenic
River near Taylors Falls.

Beaver dams are common on the backwaters and tributaries of the St. Croix River.

A resident beaver has left its impression on a tree in Wild River State Park.

Above
Storm clouds steam over bluffs on the St. Croix National Scenic River
north of the small city of Marine on St. Croix.

Facing page
Oak leaves, trees, and moss-covered boulders are scattered throughout the
Dalles region of the St. Croix National Scenic River.

Chapter 2

THE NORTH SHORE

Above
An owl feather rests on stones smoothed by
the Lake Superior surf.

Left
Lichen and sumac cling to a water-battered rock
on the North Shore of Lake Superior.

WHEN A HARD nor'easter blows, the waters of Lake Superior wash the streets of Grand Marais. The pounding surf breaches a low spit of beach gravel along the East Bay and invades the village, where folks don rubber boots and wait for the storm to pass. The legendary ferocity of Superior's storms sends waves that may top ten feet crashing against the spit. Such waves have the power to move massive shoreline boulders or break apart ships. Said to never give up its dead, Lake Superior has wrecked dozens of vessels.

The greatest of lakes, Superior is a moody neighbor with a profound influence on local weather. Summer temperatures usually stay cooler near the lake, while in winter, the mass of open water warms the shore; the lake makes ice most winters but only freezes over about once a decade. More common are immense masses of pack ice that shift with the wind on the open lake, piling along the windward shore like glittering crystal shards. Lake Superior remains numbingly cold throughout the year, with an average temperature of less than 40 degrees Fahrenheit (4°C). In the chilly environment at the water's edge, tiny arctic plants, found nowhere else in the state, grow from fissures in the black basalt.

The big lake never sleeps, rhythmically rising and falling with swells even when becalmed. Although the inland sea does not have a discernable tide, the lake level can vary several inches due to the seiche, a tide-like phenomenon triggered by wind and current. A strong blow may cause the water to "pile up" along the windward shore and cause a perceptible rise in the water level, which recedes slowly when the wind changes or subsides. A dam at the lake's outlet—the St. Mary's River at Sault Sainte Marie, Michigan—also affects the water level. Generally, the lake reaches its annual low point in early spring and then rises from the seasonal contributions of snowmelt and rain. Due to Superior's profound influence on local weather, the rugged North Shore hills receive the most snow in Minnesota. This fact is well-known to skiers, dog mushers, and other winter adventurers. Some claim the North Shore has more sled dogs per capita than any place south of Alaska!

No two views of Superior look the same, which is why the lake has long been the muse of artists and photographers. Motion, color, and light merge in a kaleidoscope of water and sky that ranges from sparkling to somber. On bitterly cold winter days, wraith-like mists dance above the lake's surface. In spring and summer, a blanket of warm air may settle over the icy water, creating a dense fog that befuddles boaters and creeps ashore, causing hazardous driving conditions on Highway 61, the North Shore Drive. Storms may occur throughout the year, though the ferocious nor'easters typically happen in early spring and late autumn. More feared by veteran boaters are the sudden summer storms that blow in from the west. Often, boaters have little warning of the approaching bad weather. Black clouds suddenly loom over the North Shore ridge, accompanied by strong, offshore winds that almost instantly create heavy seas. A boater caught out in this weather has little choice other than to make a rough run for the nearest port. In the old days, commercial fishermen would tie up to one of their nets, securely anchored in the depths, and

A brief exposure of morning sun highlights a trio of sailboats under troubled skies in Lake Superior's Grand Marais Harbor.

Lichen-encrusted boulders shelter the
Grand Marais Light Station from the
whims of Lake Superior.

ride out the blow. Occasionally, the storm would blow a fisherman far off course, and he wouldn't come to shore for hours or even days afterward, perhaps miles from his home dock.

Commercial fishing remains an integral part of Superior's mystique, but only a handful of fishing operations remain in business. The commercial fishery collapsed in the mid-twentieth century, when predation by two invasive species, combined with over-fishing, decimated native lake trout and herring stocks. Completion of the St. Lawrence Seaway in 1959 allowed sea lampreys to invade Lake Superior. These parasitic ocean eels attach themselves to living fish with a sucker-like mouth lined with sharp, rasping teeth. Once attached, lampreys literally suck the life out of their host fish. Soft-skinned lake trout proved to be easy prey for the lampreys, and extensive predation led to commercial-fishing closures during the 1960s.

The absence of lake trout, Superior's primary predator, allowed another invader, the rainbow smelt, to reach colossal abundance. This fish was introduced to inland lakes as forage for game fish in the early twentieth century; these lakes flowed to Lake Michigan, and from there the smelt spread throughout the Great Lakes. This diminutive predator is believed to have wreaked havoc on lake herring and whitefish. Though a fully grown smelt only measures seven to nine inches, they eat voraciously. Biologists believe they feed heavily on newly hatched herring and whitefish, and perhaps the eggs of these and other native species.

The recovery of Lake Superior's fishery is a conservation success story. The sea lampreys caused international concern, and the U.S. and Canadian governments worked together to fund research and control efforts. The turning point came when scientists discovered a lamprey-specific poison that could be applied to streams where the eels spawn. Regular treatments with this poison greatly reduced lamprey

All photos
Heaps, slabs, and shards of ice gather on the shoreline of Lake Superior as the warming winds of spring approach.

numbers in Superior. Barriers constructed in some rivers prevented lamprey from swimming upstream to their spawning grounds. A new generation of poisons, combined with the use of pheromones (scents) and the release of sterile males to disrupt spawning, has allowed fisheries managers to further combat lampreys in large, productive spawning areas, such as the St. Mary's River. However, sea lampreys will never be eradicated from Superior. Ongoing control programs and constant vigilance are necessary to prevent this aquatic scourge from gaining the upper hand.

Lamprey control allowed the comeback of native lake trout, and introduced trout and salmon species have flourished, too. The newly abundant trout and salmon preyed heavily upon smelt and greatly reduced their numbers, which in turn allowed herring to recover. Today, the lake seems to be returning to a natural prey-predator balance. With the restoration of wild fish, managers have discontinued most lake-trout stocking. Large-scale commercial fishing hasn't resumed, but sport fishing is the best it has been in decades.

Getting out in a boat is an excellent way to enjoy Lake Superior, whether or not you bring a fishing rod. The immensity of the lake and its ocean-like character often overwhelm first-timers. The view from the water is spectacular: brooding hills glowering over a rocky, unforgiving shore. In some areas, homes and cabins dot the shoreline, but Minnesota has fortunately retained wild shores as well. Five state parks and several waysides provide hiking trails and picnic areas at the water's edge. Growing numbers of North Shore visitors use kayaks to explore the shoreline's cliffs, coves, and cobble beaches. Near a rocky promontory called Palisade Head, relentless waves have formed caves and arches.

For the most part, the North Shore harbors few islands or sheltered bays. Near the Canadian border, the shore becomes more interesting. Rugged points reach like stony fingers into the lake. On Hat Point, at Grand Portage, a twisted cedar clings to shoreline rocks. The Witch Tree, as it is known, has been a waypoint for lakefarers for centuries. Just offshore lay the Susie Islands, a small archipelago that contains several uncommon arctic plants able to grow in the islands' chilly microclimate. Pigeon Point, at the very tip of Minnesota's Arrowhead, reaches within one mile of Minnesota's watery border with Michigan.

You don't have to go on the lake to enjoy the North Shore. The land along the shore is a popular destination for hikers, rock climbers, anglers, cross-country skiers, and other landlubbers. The forested hills are laced with ski and snowmobile trails waiting to be explored. Tumbling trout streams bounce down rocky hillsides and through forested ravines. Countless cascades surge on every river. Some are famous, like the roadside waterfalls on the Gooseberry River or the spectacular high falls on the Baptism and the Pigeon rivers. Others are known only to venturesome trout anglers or skiers who traverse frozen streams in the winter. Other natural wonders include groves of ancient cedar, windswept ridges with outstanding vistas, and lonely lakes and ponds.

An extensive network of back roads offers easy access to birders and others

Above, top
The diminutive boreal owl is a resident of northern Minnesota forests. (Photograph © Bill Marchel)

Above, bottom
Ancient indentations along the shore of Lake Superior, called Pukaskwa Pits, are thought to have been Native American storage bins or shelters.

seeking to explore the North Shore's forests, lakes, and streams. Well-known routes like the Sawbill and the Gunflint trails lead inland from Lake Superior to the edge of the Boundary Waters. Dozens of logging roads lead to secluded lakes, quiet camp-grounds, and tea-colored trout streams. In the fall, the most popular drives take place on roads near Finland, Tofte, and Lutsen that pass beneath a maple canopy ablaze in color. However, the best way to discover the North Shore's backcountry is by hiking a segment of the renowned Superior Hiking Trail, which begins in Duluth and ends near the Canadian border. The well-maintained trail follows ridge tops and river valleys, offering sweeping vistas from rock outcroppings, intimate views of secluded canyons and cascades, and pleasant woodland strolls. The trail's rugged topography often surprises first-time hikers; strong legs and sturdy footgear are required.

Travelers frequently encounter wildlife on the North Shore. Occasionally, you will see a well-fed gray wolf calmly standing on the shoulder of Highway 61. In winter, Lake Superior moderates the north country's cold temperatures, and the shore's south-facing ridges receive significantly less snow than higher elevations just a few miles inland. White-tailed deer spend the winter in yarding areas near the lake—typically, areas with dense coniferous growth. The wolves follow them, prey-ing on weakened animals and scavenging road kills. The deer population rises and falls based on the whims of weather. Mild winters make for good deer survival and lead to higher numbers the following year. Deep, lasting snows and bone-chilling temperatures cause whitetail starvation and winter kill. Most North Shore moose remain inland during the winter, where the long-legged animals can navigate deep snows. Biologists have found that moose and deer don't mix. Deer host a parasitic brain worm that doesn't affect their health; the same parasite devastates infected moose. Along the North Shore, you occasionally hear of a sickened moose that wanders into a small town or even into Duluth, seemingly oblivious of people. For safety's sake, wildlife authorities must dispatch the animal.

For birds, the North Shore serves as a major migration corridor. Every fall, birders from all over the world make pilgrimages to Hawk Ridge, on the eastern outskirts of Duluth, to watch thousands of hawks pass overhead. While many mi-gratory birds travel at night to take advantage of mild wind conditions and avoid predators, sight-hunting raptors migrate during the day, when the air is most turbu-lent. Northwest winds blow over the ridge, causing warm and cold air masses to mix and create thermals, giant bubbles of air that rise thousands of feet over the hills. Because they are large, relatively heavy birds, raptors can use the wind to conserve energy. They ride the thermals upward and then glide southward for miles. Hawks are solitary migrants, but birders often see them in large numbers at the height of migration. A collection of hawks, called a kettle, may gather over a hilltop and spiral upward on a thermal. At Hawk Ridge, the greatest numbers of hawks pass through in September. Broad-winged, sharp-shinned, red-tailed, and rough-legged hawks are among the most common migrants.

Eons of wave-induced erosion have created dozens of cobble beaches on the North Shore.

The distant Sawtooth Mountains end abruptly at Lake Superior.

While hawks are the stars of the migration show, birders can add other species to their life lists on a North Shore visit. In winter, sea ducks—including long-tailed ducks, common scoter, and harlequin ducks—can be seen in open water near Grand Marais. Owl species such as great gray owls, boreal owls, and northern hawk owls hunt in the North Shore forests. An unusual resident is the spruce grouse, commonly found in coniferous forests north of Two Harbors. The spruce grouse is the boreal neighbor of the ruffed grouse and, like many northern wildlife species, does not fear humans. The bird's trusting nature earned it the name "fool hen." However, the bird's behavior is anything but foolish. When threatened or alarmed, a spruce grouse often flutters up to perch in the dense growth of a nearby spruce or jack pine, avoiding both four-footed and winged predators.

A cynic might say the spruce grouse is foolish not to fly south each year, but many folks know that winter is one of the best times to visit the North Shore. Deep, pillowy snow arrives early and stays late. On clear winter days, conifers coated with snow stand in stunning contrast to the icy blue lake. Superior freezes slowly and generally doesn't begin making ice until February. Rarely is the ice safe for human travel, but coyotes and gray wolves commonly trot across floes a couple of hundred yards offshore. The ice affords easy travel for the wild canines during their late-winter mating season.

The March sun starts thawing snow on the south-facing slopes above Highway 61, but winter releases its grip reluctantly. Spring typically arrives with an April cloudburst of rain, sleet, and slop that beats down the snow pack, though shaded drifts may linger through May. As the melt progresses, a winter's worth of precipitation rushes toward the lake. Rivulets become rivers. Rivers become torrents. Frothing and foaming, the raging flows pitch off rocky cascades and roar through dark canyons. This is the best time to view the North Shore's famous waterfalls, though few folks see the spectacular display. Even on spring weekends, you have the state parks and hiking trails to yourself.

Summertime is a different story. While the rest of the Midwest swelters in corn-growing heat, cool Lake Superior breezes air-condition the North Shore. Summer vacationers flock to the shore, as they have for over a hundred years. They come to see the waterfalls on the Gooseberry River, to pitch a tent beside Lake Superior, to walk a forest path, or simply to relax and enjoy the cool climate. Although state parks and other stops along Highway 61 can seem crowded, even at the peak of the season you rarely have to go far to find solitude. The abundance of public land and an ever-growing recreational infrastructure provide nearly unlimited opportunities to enjoy the outdoors.

Though most vacationers never leave solid ground, it is the greatest of lakes that draws them here. Sparkling in the sun, gloomy in the rain, Superior is a commanding presence—a great inland sea at the heart of the continent.

The sacred Spirit-Little-Cedar Tree, also called the Witch Tree, has been a sentinel on Hat Point near the Canadian border for four hundred years.

Both photos
The golden glow of early morning sun highlights autumn colors on the
rugged shoreline of Lake Superior.

Above
Crashing waves create a ghost-like effect
on the North Shore.

Left
A full moon rises over Lake Superior and
Split Rock Lighthouse.

Left
Broad-winged hawks are common autumn migrants
in the skies above Duluth's Hawk Ridge.
(Photograph © Bill Marchel)

Facing page and below
At Tettegouche State Park, the high falls of the Baptism
River tumble sixty feet en route to Lake Superior.

Above
Assorted rocks and stones, worn smooth over time by the surf, rest above and below the water.

Facing page
Perhaps nowhere in Minnesota is the view of Lake Superior as grand as on top of Palisade Head, a three-hundred-foot cliff rising up from the rocky shore of the world's largest freshwater lake.

Above, top
A great grey owl glides over snow seeking the small rodents
upon which it preys. (Photograph © Bill Marchel)

Above, bottom
White-tailed deer winter near Lake Superior to take
advantage of a milder, lake-influenced climate.
(Photograph © Bill Marchel)

Right
Wave-driven water, blown and frozen solid by high winds,
blankets conifers on the North Shore near Silver Bay.

Above
Pink reflections reveal the details in bedrock submerged in Lake Superior near Grand Marais.

Left
A predawn glow reflects off boulders along the shore of Lake Superior.

Chapter 3

LAND OF LAKES

Above
Tree-topped islands lead to the distant shore
of Birch Lake in the canoe country's
Bear Island State Forest.

Left
Lily pads and bulrushes adorn northeastern
Minnesota's Echo Lake at Moose Lake State Park.

I F YOU LOOK closely among the pebbles on a sandy lake beach, you may find tiny bits of fired clay, pieces of pottery that are hundreds, or even thousands, of years old. From the earliest times, people have lived beside Minnesota's lakes. The water provides sustenance: fish, wild rice, ducks, and more. Even today, most of the state's Ojibwe communities live on the shores of major water bodies like Red Lake, Leech Lake, Mille Lacs Lake, and Lake Vermilion. But we are all drawn to the water. Lakes large and small figure prominently in our collective identity as Minnesotans, because so many of us spend our free time "at the lake"—swimming, fishing, paddling, or just plain relaxing. A dry Minnesota is incomprehensible.

Though the old slogan calls Minnesota "the Land of 10,000 Lakes," the actual total depends on who does the counting. The state fisheries program manages about five thousand lakes for fishing. Geographers say the state has about twelve thousand lakes, a total that includes waters too shallow to support game fish. These "lakes" vary from the crystalline waters of the Boundary Waters to the potholes of the western prairie. Scientists place lakes in three categories, based on their biological productivity. The deep, clear waters of the canoe country are oligotrophic, or "young," lakes, with few nutrients and minimal aquatic vegetation. Mesotrophic, or "middle-aged," lakes in the cabin country of north-central Minnesota have more nutrients and hence more vegetative growth beneath the surface and in shoreline shallows. A shallow prairie basin is an example of a eutrophic, or "old," lake with high nutrient loads and dense vegetation or algal growth. Eutrophication, the aging process of a lake, occurs naturally. Slowly, over millennia, bottom sediments accumulate and the lake fills in. The process eventually turns a shallow basin into a marsh or bog.

The most interesting aspects of a lake lie beneath the surface, where the aquatic

Right
Cattails create a mosaic of patterns in the Agassiz National Wildlife Refuge in northwestern Minnesota.

Facing page
Marshland and oaks occupy much of the Carlos Avery State Wildlife Management Area in eastern Minnesota.

ecosystem thrives in what is, to us, an alien environment. Although humans cannot breathe underwater, it's not for lack of oxygen. Aquatic life depends on the oxygen dissolved in water. During the summer, lakes stratify, with a layer of the warmest, least dense water on the surface. The water temperature decreases as you go deeper and reaches its coolest point at the thermocline, below which the water doesn't contain dissolved oxygen. Life occurs above the thermocline. When frosty autumn nights chill the surface waters, a process called turnover occurs. As the surface water cools to the same temperature as the water beneath the thermocline, the waters mix. The lake then has consistent water temperatures and dissolved oxygen levels throughout.

Morning sun highlights the shoreline of Mille Lacs Lake at Father Hennepin State Park.

In a state where nearly everyone owns a fishing rod, lake ecosystems are best described by their primary fish species. The oligotrophic lakes of the north support coldwater fish such as lake trout, whitefish, cisco, and white sucker. In the heat of summer, these species retreat to deep water above the thermocline, where the cold, infertile water contains ample amounts of dissolved oxygen. Lake trout have rigid habitat requirements and naturally occur in about a hundred inland lakes, mostly located along the Canadian border in northeastern Minnesota. Whitefish and cisco widely inhabit large, northern lakes. Whitefish abound in Upper and Lower Red Lake, and the famous Mille Lacs tullibee actually is a cisco.

Walleye, the state fish, fall into the category of cool-water species. Although walleyes are native to many waters, fish stocking to benefit anglers has introduced the species to lakes statewide. Even longtime anglers often express surprise when they discover that walleyes are not native to most of the canoe country but were initially stocked by early tourism promoters. Three hundred miles away, regular stockings on southwestern prairie lakes support a popular sport fishery. Prime natural walleye habitat is a large lake with a windswept shoreline where wave action sweeps away sediment and debris from gravel and cobble spawning areas. The size of a lake's spawning area often determines walleye abundance. Biologists describe large, windy basins like Mille Lacs Lake and Lake Winnibigoshish as walleye "factories." Walleyes have two near relatives, sauger and yellow perch. Sauger grow smaller than walleyes and primarily inhabit large systems like the lower Mississippi River and Lake of the Woods. Yellow perch occur commonly in lakes statewide and serve as an important prey species for walleyes.

Northern pike and muskellunge make up the top predators in most Minnesota lake food chains. Fanciful fishing writers often refer to pike and muskies as "water wolves," though these solitary predators neither hunt in packs nor howl at the moon. Pike are the state's most widely distributed game fish and exist nearly everywhere, from the prairie to the north woods. They may grow to large sizes, reaching twenty pounds or more, though the average Minnesota pike weighs less than five pounds. The lakes of the Upper Mississippi watershed produce some of North America's largest muskies, reaching weights of forty pounds or more. Although their natural distribution in Minnesota is mostly limited to the Mississippi drainage and Lake of the Woods, muskie have been stocked in dozens of state lakes for trophy-fishing opportunities.

Fisheries scientists describe many small and mid-sized mesotrophic lakes in the central part of the state as bass/panfish waters. Largemouth bass, bluegills, sunfish, and crappies are related species that tolerate warmer water and have different spawning habitat requirements than walleyes. Members of this piscine clan are nest-builders. Using its tail and body, the spawning fish fans off silt and sediments from a pan-shaped area on a hard lake bottom. After spawning, the male guards the nest to ward off predators. Many folks know about these spawning rituals, because bass and bluegills commonly perform them in dockside shallows during May and June.

In many respects, a healthy mesotrophic lake represents the "typical" lake ecosystem. Along the shoreline, painted turtles bask on fallen logs and kingfishers chatter from the treetops. Blue herons stalk the weedy shallows, hunting swarms of tadpoles wiggling along the sandy bottom. At dawn and dusk, bullfrogs croak like amphibian bassoonists and mallard ducklings dabble beneath the watchful eye of mother hen. Along the outer edge of the aquatic vegetation, schools of bluegills cruise like teens at a shopping mall, while bass and pike lurk in ambush.

A eutrophic lake is likely weedier, shallower, and lacking in the diversity of fish species. Bullheads and buffalo fish replace the bass and walleyes, especially as you move to the prairie. The dense growth of aquatic vegetation, while undesirable to swimmers and boaters, attracts migrating waterfowl. Wild celery, sago pondweed, and other native plants provide fuel for southbound waterfowl, which return to the same lakes year after year. Birders and bird hunters frequent waters such as Ashby's Lake Christina in west-central Minnesota, where migrating canvasback ducks gather every autumn.

Autumn colors reflect on Loon Lake in northern Minnesota's Savanna Portage State Park.

However, Christina also sets an example of how humans may accelerate the eutrophication process. In recent decades, wildlife managers have used various methods to kill off carp and other fish from Christina to improve water quality and restore the aquatic vegetation that attracts ducks. Carp are a Eurasian species introduced to Minnesota over a hundred years ago in the hopes of establishing a new fish for food and sport. The introduction succeeded immensely—carp flourished. Unfortunately, carp proved to be a pest rather than a positive addition to our biota. The prolific spawners infested rivers and lakes, often edging out native species. On the prairie, carp followed ditch systems into wetlands and shallow lakes, where they destroyed vegetation and muddied the waters. Water clarity is essential for a healthy lake, because it allows sunlight to penetrate and stimulate plant growth. Turbid water stifles vegetation and leads to summer algae blooms, exacerbating the situation. Fishery managers have attempted to remove the carp, which are usually abundant, as well as prevent their return, usually by constructing a fish barrier at the lake outlet. However, carp are tenacious,

Slabs of etched rock reflect the morning light on Lake of the Woods, the northernmost point in the state.

difficult to eradicate by poison or other means, and the extensive network of ditches often gives them avenues to return to the water body where they were eliminated. For better or worse, carp are a fixture in our aquatic ecosystems.

Seasonal cabins or homes line the shores of many Minnesota lakes, leading to the proverbial weekender expressions of "at the lake" and "up north." Unfortunately, our weekend retreats displace vital wildlife habitat, reducing or even eliminating the shoreline zone used by spawning fish, nesting birds, reptiles and amphibians, and small mammals. Runoff from lawns, agricultural fields, roads, and failing septic systems delivers nutrients and sediments that diminish lake-water quality and cause algae blooms and other pollution problems associated with eutrophication. To create a swimming beach, residents poison or uproot aquatic vegetation and then smother the natural lake bottom with sand, wiping out the places where bluegills spawn and bullfrogs croak. On many lakes, bulrush beds, floating bogs, and other natural features have disappeared as well-intentioned but woefully misguided property owners have made "their" lakes more people-friendly.

The wild persists, even on developed lakes, and it is embodied in the wavering call of Minnesota's state bird, the common loon. Loons make familiar summer residents on lakes throughout northern and central Minnesota. An estimated twelve thousand birds live statewide—the most of any state outside Alaska—and seem to be holding their own in spite of increasing human use of lake habitat. When swimming, loons form the picture of grace. Twice the size of a mallard, a loon rides low on the water, with just a couple inches of its back showing above the surface. Its most distinctive feature is a long beak that tapers to a sharp point, an effective tool for capturing fish, crayfish, leeches, and other aquatic animals. With webbed feet located far back on its body, a loon moves awkwardly on land but swims and dives excellently. A hunting loon can dive 250 feet beneath the surface in search of prey. Unlike most birds, which have hollow bones, loons have solid bones that assist diving. They hunt by sight and are believed to have good underwater vision. Although they are powerful fliers, loons need up to six hundred feet of open water to make a running, flapping takeoff. Once airborne, they can reach speeds of seventy-five miles per hour.

Loons nest at the water's edge on points, islands, or floating bogs. One to three chicks hatch after an incubation period lasting twenty-nine days. The fluffy "loonlings" rely on their parents for about two months, until they are able to fly. During the summer, you may see loon babies riding on a parent's back, a strategy that protects them from underwater predators such as northern pike and snapping turtles. By summer's end, they are fully-fledged and capable of making the long flight south. It's common to see groups of loons gathering on lakes in September, staging for their migration to wintering areas on the Gulf of Mexico and the Atlantic coast. They arrive back in Minnesota shortly after ice-out. In early spring, birders often observe groups of loons lingering on newly open lakes as they wait for the ice to break up farther north.

The thought of seeing a loon anywhere other than a north-country lake seems incongruous, because they are such a familiar symbol of Minnesota's wild waters. The tremulous call of the loon is the music we hear when we visit the places we most want to be. Ancient and unfettered, the loon song is the antithesis to traffic, telephones, and televisions. It accompanies coffee brewed over an open fire or the contemplation of a wilderness sunset. Unlike many wild creatures, loons do not act shy around people. If you stay quiet and respectful, loons may approach to within a few feet of your canoe. Such encounters are powerful, personal, and humbling. Dark and gleaming, the approaching loon surrenders none of its wildness. This is a creature whose time transcends our own, as much a part of the lake as the clear water in which it swims. We are no more than visitors within its realm.

Mussel shells riddle a beach along
Lake of the Woods.

Above, top
Fishing boats witness another sunrise on Lake Lida
in western Minnesota.

Above, bottom
The Viking ship *Hjemkomst* is featured at the Heritage
Hjemkomst Interpretative Center in Moorhead.

Left
Autumn arrives on Little Long Lake in northern
Minnesota's Chippewa National Forest.

A blue morning breaks on the Thomson Reservoir just west of Duluth.

A tree leans over Sakatah Lake in southern Minnesota.

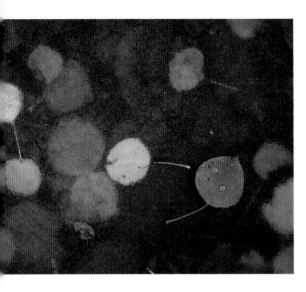

Above
Aspen leaves are temporarily suspended in ice at the Rice Lake National Wildlife Refuge in northeastern Minnesota.

Right
The Minnesota River pools up and forms Lac qui Parle in western Minnesota.

A luminous complexion reflects on Dead Horse Lake in the Chippewa National Forest.

Left, top
Remarkably, loons find places to nest and raise their young even on developed lakes. (Photograph © Bill Marchel)

Left, bottom
A loon flaps its wings dry. Loons inhabit most Minnesota lakes. (Photograph © Bill Marchel)

Far left
Autumn colors blanket the Sawtooth Mountains and Bean Lake in Tettegouche State Park.

Clouds linger over Jack the Horse Lake in the Chippewa National Forest.

An island on Albert Lea Lake, in southern Minnesota, is silhouetted against a colorful sunset.

Chapter 4

THE CANOE COUNTRY

Above
Blueberries grow in a lichen-encrusted fissure in the
Superior National Forest.

Left
A thunderstorm passes over Seagull Lake in the
Boundary Waters Canoe Area Wilderness.

ON BITTER WINTER nights, when the aspens pop from the cold and aurora borealis dance in the northern sky, howls sometimes pierce the silence of the canoe country. While the gray wolf has made a remarkable recovery throughout much of Minnesota during the last thirty years, their true stronghold lies here, beyond road's end. The wolf is a wilderness icon, a creature that symbolizes everything we cherish about the canoe country and the unspoiled north. It is no small distinction that wolves continued to thrive here after they were wiped out across the rest of the lower forty-eight. If the howl of a wolf is the song of the wild, then the canoe country is Carnegie Hall.

The heart of the canoe country is the Boundary Waters Canoe Area Wilderness, a one-million acre maze of lakes along the Canadian border and abutting Ontario's massive Quetico Provincial Park. Given permanent protection by President Jimmy Carter in 1978, the Boundary Waters is the nation's largest designated wilderness area east of the Mississippi. Most of the Boundary Waters and Quetico do not allow motors, so canoes serve as the primary mode of travel. Following historic routes, paddlers carry their canoes and packs across portage paths that link neighboring lakes. Portages vary from a few steps to more than a mile in length, but wilderness adventurers take them "in stride." Just like the Ojibwe and French voyageurs that once lived here, canoeists pitch tents at isolated campsites scattered through the wilderness. Although you are likely to encounter other people on a canoe country excursion, you'll have plenty of elbow room.

The U.S.D.A. Forest Service does not allow logging or mining in the Boundary Waters, but such was not always the case. Prospectors have explored the stony ridges and sunk exploratory shafts in the canoe country, turning up iron, copper, nickel, and even gold. In the early 1900s, workers built a railroad from Port Arthur (now Thunder Bay), Ontario, to transfer iron ore from a mine near Gunflint Lake, but the operation failed. Ely, now the primary jumping-off point for canoeists, once functioned as an iron-mining town. Long-abandoned logging roads and rail lines thread through canoe country forests; in some areas, logging continued into the 1970s. Resorts or fly-in fishing camps located on wilderness lakes were bought out by the government during the latter half of the twentieth century and dismantled or destroyed to reclaim the area's wild character. Little visible evidence remains of that era, and even less of the one preceding it—the Fur Trade. Today's canoe trails were well-traveled trade routes three hundred years ago.

Native people, most recently the Ojibwe, have called the canoe country home. A native settlement still exists on the Canadian side of Lac La Croix, but many decades have passed since native families lived in the wilderness on Canadian border lakes such as Basswood and Saganaga, where fishing and hunting formed the mainstays of their existence. From present-day place names, we know where they hunted caribou and moose or fished for suckers and sturgeon, as well as which lakes and islands held spiritual or mystic significance. Scattered like ancient graffiti on rock faces along dozens of lakes are pictographs, pigment drawings of symbols, people,

An erratic boulder nests amidst maple leaves in the Bear Island State Forest.

Cliffs loom over South Fowl Lake on the Ontario border.

animals, and mythical creatures that populated the Ojibwe world. We don't know who made the drawings, nor are they easily interpreted. Anthropologists believe some pictographs have spiritual significance, while others may simply mark the passing of a canoe party or commemorate a good hunt. Lichen-encrusted and faded with time, the pictographs are powerful reminders of the past and of another world view.

The motto for today's paddlers is "Leave No Trace," an outgrowth of a land ethic that views wilderness as a place untrammeled by man. The forest service controls access to the Boundary Waters with a daily quota on travel permits, ensuring visitors have an uncrowded experience. Canoe groups may contain no more than nine individuals—again, to reduce crowding. Some parties find a pretty campsite, set up a tent, and relax. Others seek the challenge of wilderness travel, paddling and portaging to numerous lakes. Still others come for the fishing. Boundary

Voyageurs National Park encompasses lakes laden with boulders, islands, and pine trees.

Waters lakes have world-class smallmouth bass and walleyes. Interestingly, both species were first introduced to canoe-country lakes in the early 1900s to provide sport for visiting anglers. Native fish populations include lake trout, lake whitefish, and northern pike, cold-loving species that proved difficult to catch during the summer. Walleyes and bass round out the sport fishing opportunities and provide paddlers with a reliable main course for shore lunches.

The vast majority of Boundary Waters use occurs during summer, but some hardy adventurers explore the backcountry when the lakes lie frozen and deep snows blanket the ground. Winters are harsh along the Canadian border, where nighttime lows routinely drop below -30 degrees Fahrenheit (-34°C). Actual snow depths frequently exceed three feet. Such a climate leaves little margin of error for winter visitors. Winter campers and ice fishers still rely on traditional methods of winter travel—dogsleds, snowshoes, and skis. Some outfitters even offer guided wilderness dogsled trips.

In winter, the canoe country is starkly beautiful. During the day, only the occasional croaks of soaring ravens or the cheerful chatter of chickadees break the pervasive silence. At night, when dancing northern lights illuminate the heavens and frozen trees pop like rifle shots, you may hear the wolves howl. Summer visitors may think the canoe country teams with wildlife, but the tracks in winter snow tell a different story. Relatively few warm-blooded creatures winter in the Boundary Waters. Some, like the moose, adapt especially well to the snow and cold. With a black coat of insulating hollow hair and long legs to negotiate deep snow, moose thrive in all but the most brutal winters. Another winter resident, the snowshoe hare, changes from brown to white, better concealing the animal from a host of predators. Its furry hind feet act like snowshoes (hence the name) to help it make rapid escapes in deep snow. The hare's primary predator, the Canada lynx, has furry feet, too, enabling it to follow its prey.

Some canoe-country animals spend the winter in hibernation or semi-dormancy. Black bears sleep away the winter in a den made beneath the sheltering cover of a fallen tree. Ruffed grouse dive into fluffy snow to roost, where they stay warm and secure from predators, perhaps emerging for only a couple of hours each day to feed on the buds and catkins of aspen and birch. Most active are the predators, which need to eat in order to maintain their energy levels and survive the cold. After a fresh snow, the forest floor is soon crisscrossed with the tracks of pine martens, mink-sized members of the weasel clan that relentlessly hunt red squirrels, voles, and other small mammals.

The largest predator of this northern world is the gray wolf. Living in family groups called packs, wolves efficiently hunt large prey such as moose and deer. You can frequently see wolf tracks, and occasionally wolves, on the frozen surface of canoe-country lakes. Wolf packs hunt as a team to drive deer from heavy cover or

Above
Grass grows out of a slab of submerged bedrock on Voyageurs National Park's Rainy Lake.

Left
Rapids reflect evening light on the Boundary Waters' Basswood River.

mount a lethal attack on a moose. Not every chase results in a kill. Healthy whitetails bound away to escape, and an adult moose makes a formidable opponent. Wolves frequently test their prey for signs of weakness; only the fit survive. Investigate a gathering of croaking ravens and you may discover a kill site. A wolf kill functions as a buffet luncheon for other northern creatures, though a hungry pack leaves

A mackerel sky reflects off a calm Brule Lake in the Boundary Waters.

few leftovers. Their powerful jaws crunch bones and even antlers. When the pack finishes feeding, the smaller animals arrive. Predators like red fox and pine marten search for bits of tallow and meat. Boisterous ravens announce the bounty of carnage to all who care to listen, while picking at bits and blood in the snow. Red squirrels, chickadees, shrews, and other creatures scavenge what remains and survive another winter day.

Spring comes in fits and starts. The warming-up process takes months to complete. Longer days and stronger sunlight arrive in March, raising daytime temperatures above freezing, even though they may continue to fall well below zero at night. The daily freezing and thawing forms a hard crust on the snow, perfect for skate-skiing, snowshoeing, or even walking on frozen trails. As the thaw progresses, south-facing hillsides lose their snow cover and slush forms on top of lake ice. Eventually, open water forms near inlets or narrows with current and the ice begins to rot and honeycomb. Ice-out typically arrives in late April, a time when both snowstorms and sweltering heat are climatic possibilities. Green-up is still a month away. Some Boundary Waters veterans relish the month of May, when cool weather, a lack of biting insects, and good fishing make for a pleasurable trip. Timing is everything. A hot day or warm rain may trigger the first hatch of black flies or mosquitoes—the hungriest bugs of the year!

The canoe country has a short growing season. In June, forest foliage turns vivid green and wildflowers bloom. Wobbly-legged moose calves follow their mothers to the water's edge. On portage trails, you might encounter a mother grouse feigning a broken wing as she attempts to draw intruders away from her brood of fluffy chicks. Everywhere is the promise of new life. Some years, a late frost or cold rain cuts that promise cruelly short. Life in the canoe country never comes easy, though the summer solstice is a time of plenty.

On the lakes, swarms of graceful mayflies hatch during long, midsummer evenings. Mayfly larva may spend several years living in lake-bottom silt. When conditions are right, they swim up from the bottom and emerge on the lake surface as adults. The mayfly is an elegant insect. A slender, curved body sweeps upward into a long tail comprised of three fibers as fine as a maiden's hair. Perched over the body are delicate, sail-like wings. The beauty of the bug is ephemeral. Within a day or two, the mayfly will mate and die, leaving its spent carcass floating spread-eagle on the lake. However, for other creatures, the few short days of the mayfly hatch herald a time of plenty. Walleyes, whitefish, bass, and trout gorge on the swimming nymphs and slurp the adult mayflies resting on the surface. Above the water, cedar waxwings swoop down from high perches to pluck fluttering mayflies from the gathering dusk. Long after sunset, a glow lingers in the northern sky. Somewhere beyond the canoe country shines a midnight sun.

The summer evenings already grow shorter by blueberry time. The dog days are hot, dry, and much favored by paddlers who come to the Boundary Waters to swim, sunbathe, and relax. Blueberries ripen on rock outcroppings and burned-over areas where sunlight reaches the low-growing bushes. Blueberries are the canoe country's most important wild crop. In the past, native people picked large quantities of the fat berries and dried them for winter use. Today's pickers use blueberries as the main ingredient in pies, jams, and even wines. Blueberry picking is a labor-intensive activity; a person may take an hour or more just to gather enough tiny berries for a pie. But blueberry lovers insist the sweet rewards justify the effort. Sometimes, they have competition in the berry patch; black bears are famously fond of blueberries. Trampled brush and "bear sign" indicate places where they've been feeding.

Storm clouds and snow-laden white pines loom over South Hegman Lake in the Boundary Waters.

Blueberries are what ecologists refer to as an early successional plant, a species that thrives in the wake of a forest disturbance. Native people were thought to have started occasional fires in favorite berry-picking areas to clear out competing trees and brush. The open areas likely created browsing areas for woodland caribou (now absent from the area) and moose. Fire remains an important component of the canoe-country ecosystem. While the forest service suppresses accidental fires caused by campers, it allows naturally ignited fires (usually lightning strikes) to burn. Depending on the intensity of the blaze, a wildfire may destroy most trees or just burn through the understory. Large, fire-resistant trees such as white pine may survive several fires during the course of their two-hundred-year-plus lifetime. Other trees, such as jack pine, need a hard fire to clear away the forest and create a blackened seedbed for new saplings to sprout. Typically, a large wildfire burns a mosaic pattern on the landscape. In some places, everything is destroyed, while in others, shifting winds and natural fire breaks allow patches of vegetation to survive. Ecologists can map the extent of past fires, even those that occurred centuries ago, by studying the existing vegetation. In the canoe country, for instance, a birch-cloaked hillside along a lake usually marks a place where a fire occurred decades ago. Birches are one of the first trees to grow in a burned-over area.

On July 4, 1999, a natural event occurred that will shape the canoe country far into the future. A fierce thunderstorm accompanied by unusually strong downbursts of wind flattened thousands of forested acres along the Canadian border from Ely eastward to the Gunflint Trail and beyond. Although the storm lasted less than an hour, the devastation left in its wake was mind-boggling. An impenetrable mess of broken, twisted, and uprooted trees stretched for miles. In many places, all that remained standing were cedar and black spruce in the lowlands and scattered white pines on the hills. Loggers salvaged some timber and cleaned up the storm damage in areas near habitation, such as along the Gunflint Trail, but most of the blow-down occurred within the Boundary Waters, where logging is not allowed. Worried about a catastrophic fire igniting the innumerable downed trees, forestry officials have started small fires in key locations to create fire breaks and reduce the fuel load. While the risk of fire has not been eliminated, they hope the planned burns will lessen the chance of an uncontrollable wildfire escaping into the wilderness. Saplings are already forcing their way through the tangled debris, the sprouting promise of a new forest.

The 1999 blow-down dramatically changed the scenery in the heart of the Boundary Waters, but farther west, Voyageurs National Park was largely unscathed by the storm. Nestled along the Canadian border, Voyageurs is mostly roadless, but the park does allow motorized travel. In the summer, fishing boats and houseboats ply the interconnected waters of Rainy, Kabetogama, Namakan, and Sand Point lakes. In winter, the frozen lakes create a snowmobiling paradise. The park's emphasis on motorized recreation attracts a different sort of adventurer than does the

Clouds drift past islands on the Superior National Forest's Ojibway Lake.

nonmotorized Boundary Waters, but the character of the country remains the same. Pine-studded islands and sinuous, unspoiled shorelines offer seclusion for camping, fishing, or relaxing, miles from the nearest road. Wolves roam the rocky ridges and, during the winter, are occasionally seen crossing the frozen lakes.

While lines on a map may separate wilderness from woods, or national park from national forest, the canoe country has continuity. Every summer, modern adventurers paddle the historic Voyageurs Highway, the primary route of fur traders three hundred years ago. The actual route begins at Grand Portage on Lake Superior and runs westward along the Canadian border to Lake of the Woods. For hundreds of years, this pathway through lakes and connecting rivers served as a busy, intercontinental highway. Native people first used the route and populated it with their camps and villages. Even today, Ojibwe communities live at Grand Portage and on the Canadian bank of Lac La Croix. Early European explorers mapped the route, which then became a major artery for the fur trade. This historical era—when teams of colorful French voyageurs sang as they paddled huge, birch-bark Montreal canoes—continues to define the canoe country. Some say you can still hear their songs in the music of a rapid river or a wind-tossed lake. Certainly, in the solitude of the wilderness, you can paddle across time.

Above, top
Boulders and white pines make a stand on the shore of Kabetogama Lake in Voyageurs National Park.

Above, bottom
Canoe country paddlers never know when they'll turn a corner and encounter a bull moose. (Photograph © Bill Marchel)

Above
Boulders lay at rest in a calm bay on Birch Lake in the
Bear Island State Forest.

Left
A bank of fog begins to dissipate on Sand Point Lake in
Voyageurs National Park.

A fog-shrouded island on Sand Point Lake reflects shades of blue and green.

The cliffs of Grassy Bay loom over Sand Point Lake.

Left
The snowshoe hare is an important prey species for canoe country predators, especially the Canada lynx. (Photograph © Bill Marchel)

Below
Fresh snow covers islands on Bear Head Lake in Bear Head Lake State Park.

Facing page
In the Bear Island State Forest, the coursing river fights off the freezing grips of winter.

Turtle Island, on Vermilion Lake, takes on different moods in different lights and seasons.

THE CANOE COUNTRY / 105

Chapter 5

THE ENDURING PRAIRIE

Above
Sioux quartzite boulders poke out of Pipestone
Creek at southwestern Minnesota's Pipestone
National Monument.

Left
Glacial erratic rocks rest on a windswept
south-central prairie.

ETHEREAL BOOMS ROLL across the prairie to greet the April dawn. In a meadow of snow-matted grass, male prairie chickens have begun their elaborate mating ritual. Shadowy forms appear in the gathering light, and each grouse takes its place. The choreograph began the previous fall, when the cocks staked claim to a few square feet of the "booming ground." Now, the dance begins. It is a spectacular natural performance.

The cock prairie chicken, an uncommonly handsome bird, displays all of his finery during the courtship ritual. Standing flat-footed, he hunches forward and fans his tail. Long neck feathers called *pinnae* stand erect over his head as he inflates two large, sunrise-orange neck sacs, producing a loud, three-note booming sound. Coming out of the booming posture, he performs a distinctive, quick-step dance that has been mimicked by the prairie's native people. Completing the dance, he hops and flutters a couple of feet into the air. If another male approaches, he scurries to the unseen but very real boundary of his territory to ward off the intruder. A booming ground may contain a dozen or more displaying cocks, all vying for attention from visiting hens. The booming sound is overwhelming.

Prairie chickens are native to Minnesota, although European settlement profoundly influenced their population and range in the state. The prairie chicken story is also the story of the Minnesota prairie, a parable of what is, what was, and what may be. Prior to settlement, prairie chickens lived in extreme southern Minnesota, while a near-relative, the sharp-tailed grouse, ranged across most of the state's prairies. As settlers struggled to tame a wild land with plow, axe, and fire, they created a landscape mosaic of pasture, prairie, and fields of small grains. Prairie chickens flourished in the newly disturbed environment. In 1900, when even northern Minnesota functioned as a "prairie" due to logging and repeated fires, the birds thrived statewide.

The prairie chicken era lasted just a few decades. Social and economic changes wrought by the Great Depression and World War II brought an end to hardscrabble farming. In the north, cleared land returned to forest, while more intensive agricultural practices eliminated pastures and grasslands in the south and west. As the grass disappeared, so did the prairie chickens. Today, a few thousand prairie chickens inhabit the Glacial Ridge grasslands, once a gravelly beach on ancient Lake Agassiz, where rocky soils and boggy wetlands have resisted the plow. No one expects Minnesota prairie chickens to return to their former abundance, but we may see more birds in the future. Agricultural conservation programs and habitat restorations, run by state and federal wildlife agencies, have helped to create new grasslands. Recent prairie chicken introduction in some of these areas show promise.

Native prairie is one of Minnesota's most precious wild resources. Less than 1 percent of the state's original eighteen to twenty million acres of prairie remains,

Tufts of fringed sage form patterns on the Nature Conservancy's Bluestem Prairie east of Moorhead.

scattered in mostly small tracts from the Mississippi River bluffs in the southeast to the aspen parklands in the northwest. Prairie once covered most of today's agricultural region, including parts of the metropolitan area. Early explorers described a sea of tall grass alive with wildlife, including bison, elk, and grizzly bears. Laced with potholes, marshes, and meandering creeks, the prairie functioned like a vast sponge—absorbing spring snowmelt and rain, then metering out clean water to feed the Minnesota, the Red, and other river systems. Prairie wetlands attracted breeding waterfowl, shorebirds, and a host of other species. During spring and fall migrations, endless strings of ducks and geese crossed the sky.

What remains of the Minnesota prairie still has birds in variety and abundance. Bird-watching, an increasingly popular activity, makes for an excellent introduction to the prairie. Whether you view marbled godwits at Salt Lake on the South Dakota border, prairie chickens at Bluestem Prairie, or sandhill cranes near Thief River Falls, birding will lead you to the state's best prairie habitat.

Agriculture, the predominant use of the landscape, influences the diversity and abundance of prairie wildlife species. Large, free-ranging mammals such as bison and wolves are gone, and only a few remnant elk exist in the northwest. White-tailed deer and coyotes, two species able to live in close proximity to humans, now fill the niche as the largest prey and predator. In intensively cultivated areas, the native prairie grouse gave way to game birds introduced from Asia and Europe—the ring-necked pheasant and Hungarian partridge—which adapt better to large-scale farming. Even common predators like raccoons and striped skunks have grown more numerous on the farmed landscape. Some native species, such as burrowing

Above
Shooting star reach for the sky in southern Minnesota.

Right
Goldenrod and button blazing star mingle with prairie grasses at Lake Bronson State Park in northwestern Minnesota.

owls and spotted skunks, disappeared from Minnesota due to habitat loss. Others, such as the prairie chickens, are holding on where suitable grassland habitat still exists.

Prior to settlement, the prairie grass grew taller than a man, which is why we call Minnesota's prairie ecosystem the Eastern Tall Grass Prairie. North America's great grasslands occur in the rain shadow of the Rocky Mountains. The landscape is arid immediately east of the mountains, but annual precipitation increases and frequency of drought decreases as you move east. By the time you reach Minnesota, ample precipitation allows the grass to grow lush and high. Some native species, including big and little bluestem, grama, Indian grass, switch grass, and prairie cord grass, typically grow to heights of three feet or more. The original prairie grasslands were maintained by grazing bison and sporadic fires, sometimes ignited by native peoples, that replenished soil nutrients and prevented the encroachment of trees and shrubs. Woody vegetation typically grew along waterways or in open, upland oak savannahs. In northwestern Minnesota, large islands of aspens growing amidst the grass form a natural system known as parklands. The transition from prairie to woodlands often occurs abruptly, though today, farmland mostly marks the prairie's edge.

Prairie appreciation is an acquired taste. Newcomers often feel struck by the apparent sameness of the surroundings—the endless grass and sky—rather than the prairie's wondrous but subtle diversity. Getting to know the prairie is like reading a book that starts out slow in the first chapter and grows more absorbing with each turn of the page. The vastness of the prairie is humbling, its minutia, endlessly fascinating. Step into the grass and let a wind spawned in Montana caress your face. Then look down to study the carpet of biodiversity, an interdependent mix of wild grasses and flowering plants that may contain dozens of species within a few square

Left
Purple coneflowers compete for space
in the Marcy-Holmes Community
Garden near the Mississippi River
in Minneapolis.

Below
Pastel-colored bent grass covers the
edge of a marsh in central Minnesota's
Sherburne National Wildlife Refuge.

feet. Depending upon the season, various flowers may be in bloom. First to appear in early spring are the tiny pasqueflowers. Summer brings a burst of color from blazing star, prairie smoke, and prairie fringed orchid. Bright yellows predominate as autumn approaches from the blooms of goldenrod, the uncommon compass plant, and other species. Among the wildflowers, butterflies bask in their own brilliance. Some butterfly species, such as the Dakota skipper, Karner blue, and regal fritillary, need intact prairie habitat to survive and serve as bellwethers of a healthy grassland ecosystem.

Fire remains an essential element of the prairie. In early spring, plumes of smoke billow on the horizon as land managers set fire to prairie preserves. Trained fire-fighting crews control the course of the blaze and prevent it from escaping to other properties. The fire ripples through the dry vegetation, burning the thatch of dead grasses and debris and killing woody shrubs and saplings. Within days, new growth turns the blackened land green and fresh. Land managers set intentional fires as a management tool, as did native people before them. But wild fires have always been a primal element of the prairie ecosystem. Historically, lightning strikes ignited periodic fires. The fires set back the process of natural succession and prevented brush and trees from overtaking a grassland. The lush growth that sprouted after a fire provided nourishment for grazing animals such as bison and better cover for ground-nesting birds. Today's controlled burns serve the same ecological purpose, albeit on a smaller scale.

Ironically, the only way we can retain a semblance of wild prairie is through continued human stewardship, but therein lies the future's promise. Agricultural science is being used to bring back the wild grasses. Using seeds from locally grown "crops" of grass, prairie managers re-establish native vegetation on abandoned and marginal farmland. The resulting fields of big bluestem, Indian grass, and grama lack the species diversity of original prairie, though the source seeds usually contain a few native wildflowers. Over time, it is hoped the vegetation established on the new grasslands will replicate the prairie ecosystem and create new reserves for native species.

While only scattered puddles of Minnesota's once-vast sea of grass remain, prairie ghosts linger. At sunset, when the dying breeze whispers in the grass, you can encounter these ghosts. Climb the windswept ridges of Blue Mounds State Park, where prickly pear cactus finds a foothold on the arid bluffs, and run your hands across the ancient face of boulders worn from the rubbing of long-vanished bison. Contemplate the symbols and imagery etched in the stone outcroppings at Jeffers Petroglyphs Historic Site, an indelible record left by peoples who once roamed the wild prairie. At Pipestone National Monument, watch their descendants quarry soft carving stones from ancient trench mines—a right preserved in federal treaties. The sound of their work is an echo of the wild past. We are privileged to listen.

Facing page
Lone oak trees stand in a state of nature on the central Minnesota landscape.

Above, top
A cock prairie chicken, with air sacs inflated and pinnae erect, performs a mating ritual as ancient as the prairie. (Photograph © Bill Marchel)

Above, bottom
An ancient thunderbird petroglyph is carved in quartzite at the Jeffers Petroglyphs State Historic Site in southwestern Minnesota.

Left
In the state's southwest corner at Blue Mounds State Park, early light warms the Sioux quartzite rock cliffs.

The rolling glacial landscape of the Leaf Hills pops up through morning fog in west-central Minnesota.

A pair of oak trees face the morning at the Sherburne National Wildlife Refuge.

A storm front moves over the southwestern prairie and Sioux quartzite boulders embedded at Blue Mounds State Park.

Left
A whitetail buck and doe bound across the prairie, where they have replaced the elk and bison once found here. (Photograph © Bill Marchel)

Below
Bluestem prairie grasses and aspen trees thrive on what is known as the aspen parkland in and around Lake Bronson State Park.

The earth gradually reclaims mechanical dinosaurs and other relics of the past in central Minnesota.

Big bluestem and wind-sculpted snow adorn a south-central prairie near historic Fort Ridgely.

Above
A monarch butterfly rests on blazing star.
(Photograph © Bill Marchel)

Left
Prairie blazing star thrive in the Nature
Conservancy's Bluestem Prairie in west-central Minnesota.

A glacially formed landscape, featuring kames, kettles, eskers and moraines, occupies
much of Glacial Lakes State Park in central Minnesota.

A forgotten farmhouse faces threatening skies in southwestern Minnesota.

Chapter 6

FOREST REALMS

Above
The pileated woodpecker needs old, decaying
trees to find food and build its nest.
(Photograph © Bill Marchel)

Left
Deciduous and coniferous trees mingle in the
Superior National Forest in northern Minnesota.

IN THE HEART of the Lost Forty, you can find the Minnesota primeval. Tall pines, their trunks like pillars in a cathedral, are the majestic remnants of the great pineries that once stretched from the St. Croix River valley to the Canadian border. Located in the Chippewa National Forest in northern Itasca County, the Lost Forty exists because of a surveyor's error a century ago, when Minnesota's original pine forests were cut down to meet a growing nation's demand for lumber. The over-looked grove of white and red pines provides a glimpse of history. When a soft wind blows, you can hear the ancient whispers of a ghost forest.

Pre-settlement Minnesota had a wealth of wood measured not only in pines but also in the fat oaks of the prairie savannahs, the black spruce and tamarack bogs of the north, the maples and basswoods of the Big Woods, and the hickories and black walnuts of the bluff country. During the past 150 years, nearly all of Minnesota's forests have been altered by intensive human activity, including logging, land-clearing for agriculture, urban sprawl, and recreational development. Yet the forest endures. Most Minnesota woodlands are of wild origin, the natural regeneration of native species. What has changed is the age and abundance of various tree species. White pines, for instance, remain a familiar sight—as solitary trees.

Today's forests are dominated by short-lived species such as aspen and birch, which generally sprout first following a major disturbance. The settlement era wiped much of the state clean of forest vegetation. In the north, logging preceded devastating slash fires that blackened vast areas. Central-Minnesota settlers in pursuit of Manifest Destiny pulled stumps and broke ground for agriculture. Massive erosion resulted from attempts to farm steep hillsides in the southeast. Visionaries such as the late Richard Dorer, leader of the old Minnesota Department of Conservation, encouraged the reforestation of denuded and often tax-forfeit lands. We owe our present wealth of public forests to their efforts.

Wind and fire shaped the pre-settlement forest. Periodic blow-downs and wildfires created a landscape mosaic that included everything from saplings to centuries-old pines and cedars. Although we now have the capability to suppress most wildfires, natural disturbances such as wind-storms, insects, and disease still influence our forests. However, harvesting to supply the forest-products industry has largely supplanted wildfire as the primary disturbance. Forest managers use state-of-the-art harvesting and silvi-culture techniques to minimize ecological damage and mimic natural processes.

Throughout the various disturbance regimes, the forest has remained dynamic. Since forests change slowly, over a span of decades or even centuries, the casual observer hardly notices the progression of what ecologists call natural succession. Following a disturbance that removes some or all of the standing trees in a wooded area, new growth sprouts from the earth. In northern Minnesota, aspen and birch saplings appear first, because they grow well in full sunlight. Jack pine grows after

Both photos
The cool air and short days of autumn bring out a pallet of color in the Superior National Forest.

the heat from a fire opens its hard cones and releases the seeds. These early successional species are relatively short-lived, with lifespans ranging from 60 to 120 years. During that time, shade-tolerant species such as balsam fir and white spruce come up under the aspen and birch canopy. Longer-lived trees, such as white pine and red pine, may sprout in sunlit openings.

Resistant to fire and wind, large white pine and red pine often survive disturbances that level neighboring trees and restart the successional process. Preferring moist ground, massive white cedars dominate deeply shaded groves. These stands of cedar cool and filter surface water destined for trout streams and walleye lakes. Cedars and the tall pine species may live for several hundred years. Ironically, these old-growth species have the hardest time getting a start in Minnesota's woods. White-tailed deer—rare in the original old-growth pine forests but common in birch and aspen woods—browse heavily on pine and cedar saplings. Blister rust, an Old World disease that invaded Minnesota a century ago, disfigures and eventually kills white pines. Economic impatience also works against the old-growth trees. A ready market exists for species that reach merchantable size in forty to eighty years, dampening the incentive to manage forests for trees that live centuries.

The state does not manage all of Minnesota's forests for commercial use. Over one million acres of public forests are reserved from logging as parks, preserves, and wilderness land. Even within "working forests," management plans chart a course far into the future. Just as previous generations of foresters and conservationists took steps to protect and restore the forests we enjoy today, future Minnesotans will benefit from the plans guiding the modern management of public forests. Today's forest managers use new silvicultural techniques to restore white pines in places where the timber once grew tall. Wildlife habitat, aesthetics, and recreation receive serious consideration in the planning process and when logging occurs. Independent "green" certification of Minnesota's forest products ensure that managers use state-of-the-art, sustainable forestry practices. Long-term management plans ensure that we do not repeat the past plundering of the lumber barons.

We can take hope from the work of planners, but plans are made on tabletops. The forest we experience is immediate and real. In Minnesota, we call it "the woods," whether it is a maple-basswood ridge west of Hill City, a black walnut and hickory grove east of Lanesboro, or a broomstick aspen thicket north of Two Harbors. A forest is a place with trees. The woods are more personal. We go for walks, wander back roads, fish for trout, and hunt deer in the woods. When you spend time outdoors in Minnesota, if you are not on a lake, you are most likely in the woods.

Ecologists call our woods "biologically bland" compared with the diverse vegetation in more temperate climes. But Minnesota sits at the crossroads for the forests of eastern North America. The boreal forest extends southward from Canada like a finger following the cool-climate edge of the North Shore. In the comparatively balmy shelter of the Mississippi and the St. Croix river valleys, southern species creep as far north as Minnesota winters allow. Like a high-water mark of Atlantic influence, eastern hemlock reaches the westernmost extent of its range in the vicinity of Jay Cooke State Park, south of Duluth.

Nature reclaims a pioneer cemetery in Itasca State Park.

Minnesota Highway 23, running an hour south from Jay Cooke to the town of Sandstone, offers a windshield view of the merging forests. After crossing the St. Louis River at Fond du Lac, the highway passes through forest comprised of boreal tree species such birch, aspen, and balsam. Northern white oaks appear as you continue south. A few jack pines, born in the aftermath of savage fires that scarred the land nearly one hundred years ago, as well as some white pines, survivors of the same, occur in scattered clusters in the sandy uplands. When the highway descends into the Kettle River valley, the view of hardwoods is not so different from what you might see along a river in Missouri. The boreal forest has been left behind.

Perhaps better than trees, wildlife defines the boundary between north and south. Moose, for instance, primarily inhabit northern-tier counties where the snow piles too deep for deer in the winter and, more importantly, where summers stay consistently cool. In the forest, gray squirrels only venture as far north as they can find acorns, though "townies" seem able to survive wherever there are bird feeders. Snowshoe hares once ranged as far south as northern Anoka County, just north of the Twin Cities, but biologists have charted a slow, northward regression of their range in recent decades. At the same time, the opossum, which once inhabited only extreme southern Minnesota, now has been documented as far north as Grand Rapids. Another southern species, the wild turkey, has been successfully introduced as far north as Brainerd.

Ruffed grouse, the signature species of Minnesota woodlands, inhabit forests from the Iowa border to Ontario. Researchers have discovered that the ruffed-

Above, top
The forests along the North Shore harbor patches
of various colored lupines.

Above, bottom
A yellow lady slipper stands out in Itasca State Park.

Above, top
A lone pink lupine stands in a sea of purple lupines
near the North Shore.

Above, bottom
White trillium blanket the forest floor in the Blackhoof
River State Wildlife Management Area.

grouse range closely overlaps that of aspen, a tree more common in Minnesota than any other state. Aspen forests blanket much of northern Minnesota, where the tree is prized as a species that quickly regenerates after logging and provides excellent habitat for a range of wildlife species. Though less commonly, aspen also occurs along field edges and newly logged areas in the southeastern bluff country.

Wherever you find aspen, you can expect to find grouse nearby. In various life stages, from sapling to mature tree, aspen provide grouse with cover and food. During the nesting season, grouse hens rear their broods in the dense cover of young aspens. The aspen is what botanists call dioecious, meaning separate trees have male or female reproductive parts, and in winter, grouse feed heavily on the buds of male aspen trees. Uniquely adapted to survive brutal northern winters, ruffed grouse roost in snow burrows. The snow insulates the birds from the cold and hides them from predators. During the depths of winter, grouse may spend nearly all of their time beneath the snow, emerging only at dusk to feed on buds and catkins in the treetops.

All photos
New growth begins on the forest floor following a wildfire in the Itasca Wilderness Sanctuary. Some of the oldest red and white pines in Minnesota live in Itasca State Park.

The abundance of ruffed grouse follows a natural cycle as mysterious as it is predictable. Every spring, just after the snow melts, biologists make daybreak drives through the woods to listen for male grouse, or "drummers." To attract mates, a male takes up position on a fallen log and announces his presence to prospective hens by rapidly beating his wings for several seconds. The rush of air creates a drumming sound, which some folks liken to the roar of starting up a small engine. By driving the same routes year after year and recording the number of drummers they hear, biologists derive a reasonable and consistent estimate of grouse abundance. In the span of a decade, ruffed grouse numbers will increase until the birds seem to be everywhere and then, within two or three years, decline to scarcity. Minnesota wildlife managers have long documented the cycle, but they cannot explain what triggers the rise and fall in grouse numbers. Some believe aspens produce a toxin in reaction to abundant grouse over-eating their buds, while others postulate the decline is due to a cyclical increase in goshawks or other predators. Some even say the grouse cycle is related to sunspot activity!

For many folks more accustomed to sidewalks than footpaths, the forest itself is a mystery. The fear of being lost in the woods is embedded deep within our mainstream culture. Early settlers regarded the forest as a foreboding, almost supernatural, entity. Clearing the forest and "taming" the wilderness took on a near-religious significance as the end product of Manifest Destiny. While we've long since learned to appreciate and manage forests, the fear of the woods persists. Outside of the Boundary Waters, precious few places remain in Minnesota where you can wander the forest without encountering a logging road, snowmobile route, hiking trail, or some other human pathway. However, this reality hasn't slowed the sales of compasses or global positioning units. Perhaps old fears are hard to overcome. Or maybe we'd rather believe in a mythical, wild woods, a place where we can disappear amidst the trees.

Above, top
The historic North West Company Fur Post, near Pine City, has been reconstructed to depict a wilder time in Minnesota's past.

Above, bottom
Fox tracks wander across a frozen marsh in the St. Croix River valley.

Clouds drift over red pines in northern Minnesota's Tamarac National Wildlife Refuge.

Left, top
The ruffed grouse and its characteristic drumming ritual is a sound of spring in Minnesota forests. (Photograph © Bill Marchel)

Left, bottom
Whitetails abound in the state's hardwood forests. (Photograph © Bill Marchel)

Far left
Bracken ferns and aspens prepare for winter in the Arrowhead region.

Hoarfrost covers an oak savannah in east-central Minnesota.

Morning light creates shadows on Boulder Lake in the Cloquet State Forest in northeastern Minnesota.

Both photos
The Superior Hiking Trail runs through the Sawtooth Mountains and along the ridgeline of Lake Superior.

Above, top
Maple leaves form a pool in Mille Lacs Kathio State Park.

Above, bottom
White pine needles, aspen leaves, and cedar sprigs float
near the Cascade River.

Above, top
Bare branches reflect in a pool of maple leaves in
Mille Lacs Kathio State Park.

Above, bottom
Oak and maple leaves carpet new snow at Wild River State Park.

Sugar maple leaves change color in the Chengwatana State Forest.

Above
Aspens glow under mackerel skies in north-central Minnesota.

Facing page
Aspens reach for the sky at Tettegouche State Park on the North Shore.

Chapter 7

A Passion for the Wild

Minnesota's Conservation Legacy

Above
Bigtooth aspen leaves and white pine needles rest on
the forest floor in Savanna Portage State Park.

Left
Piebald skies loom over Caribou Lake and the
Sawtooth Mountains in the Arrowhead region.

MINNESOTA IS NOT wild by accident. Throughout this book, we've visited places where the wild exists and natural communities are comprised of native plants and animals. We are fortunate to live in a state with a wealth of wild places—the Boundary Waters, state parks and natural areas, national wildlife refuges, public forests, undeveloped lakes, and untamed rivers. Collectively, these places represent a legacy passed on to us by previous generations of conservationists. We live in a state where people have long appreciated wild lands and fought to protect them. The creation of the Chippewa National Forest, the Agassiz National Wildlife Refuge, and the Boundary Waters did not occur by happenstance. Individuals and organizations believed that saving the wild was the right thing to do. They wrote letters, attended meetings, battled industries and economic interests, and, ultimately, prevailed in politics to legislate long-term protection of our state's most outstanding natural resources.

The newest addition to this legacy is the 35,000-acre Glacial Ridge National Wildlife Refuge, created in 2004. Located in northwest Minnesota, southeast of Crookston, Glacial Ridge exemplifies what is and what can be. Once a stony prairie interspersed with shallow wetlands, the area was used for decades to graze cattle as a private ranch operation. Later, a corporate agribusiness obtained government subsidies to dig a network of ditches throughout the property in an attempt to drain the wetlands and break the prairie sod for row-crop farming. Ultimately, the rocky soil proved better suited to growing grass than grain. Since the property had limited agricultural potential, The Nature Conservancy was able to acquire it. Slowly, the task of restoration began.

Working with an array of government natural resource agencies and non-profit conservation organizations, and with the support of the local community, the conservancy planted native grasses in former farm fields and plugged ditches to fill long-dry potholes. The work benefited not only wildlife, ranging from prairie chickens to moose, but also the region's human inhabitants. The restored wetlands act as water-retention basins for the flood-prone Red River valley. The wells for Crookston's water are located on prairie uplands within the refuge, which should protect the aquifer from contamination or water loss to nearby competing wells.

Few would disagree that the establishment of Glacial Ridge National Wildlife Refuge was a win-win endeavor for wildlife and people. In a state where less than 1 percent of the original prairie remains, such large-scale grassland restoration represents a tremendous accomplishment—and one, unfortunately, difficult to repeat in other locales. The Glacial Ridge project became possible only after the land proved largely unsuitable for farming or development. Elsewhere in the state, land that was once prairie and potholes has been converted to productive farmland or suburban subdivisions. The wild prairie trickled away, the victim of a century of drainage projects. In Minnesota, drain tiles underlay many crop fields, whisking runoff to ditches and creeks, then on to major river systems. Draining projects have eradicated nearly all of the state's prairie wetlands, compounding the effects of pollution

An abandoned farmhouse is framed through a barn door in southwestern Minnesota.

and flooding farther downstream. The origin of a barren, oxygen-depleted zone in the Gulf of Mexico can be traced to the Minnesota River, where agricultural runoff and sewage contribute to polluting nutrient loads.

Recent conservation efforts, notably federal subsidies that encourage the conversion of marginal and erosion-prone cropland to natural cover, have improved water quality. But these efforts haven't countered the effects of wetland loss throughout the watershed. Most prairie and wetland restorations are small-scale projects, generally a few hundred acres or less. Acquiring former farms from willing sellers or donors, public agencies have created hundreds of wildlife areas, islands of restored habitat amidst a sea of plowed earth. But experts say the only way to truly restore the wild is to establish federal incentives for farmers to permanently retire vast tracts of less productive farmland rather than cultivating every available acre. Declining water quality may create the political imperative needed to change farm programs. Minnesota Pollution Control Agency tests have found many farmland waterways do not meet the "fishable and swimmable" criteria of the national Clean Water Act. The state must take steps to clean up these "impaired waters" or face eventual federal regulatory action.

An erratic boulder settles on the Bonanza Prairie along Big Stone Lake in western Minnesota.

White pines line the shore of Kabetogama Lake in Voyageurs National Park.

Dirty water poses a problem statewide. Many small communities have inadequate sewage treatment facilities and cannot afford necessary upgrades. Non-permeable surfaces—roads, roofs, and parking lots—alter the flow, temperature, and quality of urban runoff. Coal-fired power plants in distant states discharge airborne pollutants that contaminate rain and snow, entering some of Minnesota's most pristine waters. The Minnesota Department of Public Health issues fish-consumption warnings due to the accumulation of mercury in predator species such as walleyes and lake trout, even those taken from lakes within the Boundary Waters. In many other lakes, shoreline house and cottage development contributes nutrients to the water, leading to unnatural summer algae blooms. On the North Shore, land-clearing and road-building associated with residential development have made once-cold creeks too warm to support trout. Beaches on Lake Superior are closed to swimming due to E. coli contamination. The Mississippi River, pristine as it splashes over the rocks at the outlet of Lake Itasca, becomes an alphabet soup of contaminants below the Twin Cities.

In addition to chemical pollution, Minnesota waters host a variety of plants and animals that don't belong here. Invasive species such as zebra mussels, Eurasian water milfoil, and round gobies compromise native ecosystems. Hitchhiking in the ballast water of commercial freighters, zebra mussels entered the Great Lakes ecosystem and then spread to other waters. The thumbnail-sized clams adhere to hard surfaces ranging from submerged rocks to boat hulls in mind-boggling abundance. As filter feeders, zebra mussels prey upon the microscopic plants and animals that form the base of the aquatic food chain. They affect their new environment so profoundly that turbid waters such as the Mississippi's Lake Pepin have become clearer since their infestation. The zebra mussel plague has largely spared icy Lake Superior because the tiny clams prefer more temperate waters. However, zebra mussels, along with several other invasive species, have become established in the Duluth Harbor, a busy international port. Biologists worry that the mussels and two small, exotic fish found in the harbor, the round goby and the river ruffe, could inadvertently spread to inland waters via boaters or anglers. They have good reason for their concern. Plant fragments stuck to boats and trailers allowed Eurasian water milfoil to spread to dozens of Minnesota lakes since the plant first appeared in Lake Minnetonka in 1987.

Once invasive species become established, control efforts often prove impossible or prohibitively expensive. One of the more successful efforts has been the fight against a colorful plant called purple loosestrife, which took root in shallow wetlands throughout the state and overwhelmed native vegetation. After testing, biologists introduced beetles that specifically preyed upon purple loosestrife, greatly reducing the plant's abundance but not eliminating it. More often, natural-resource managers must use herbicides or pesticides to control unwanted species.

Some exotic species are so well-established on land or in water that we scarcely recognize them as nonnative. Carp and buckthorn exemplify long-established invasive species from the Old World. Another is the common earthworm or night crawler. In recent years, ecologists have found that earthworms feed voraciously on the layer of decaying materials, called duff, that covers the floor of north-central Minnesota's hardwood forests, causing the loss of tree seedlings, wildflowers, and ferns.

On the flip side of the ecological coin are Minnesota's endangered, threatened, and uncommon species. These native plants and animals face a tenuous existence due to limited or disappearing habitat or other circumstances. Since Minnesota lies at a crossroads of landscapes and ecosystems, some species are naturally rare or unusual, such as the arctic plants growing on the shores of Lake Superior. Others—particularly grassland species such as burrowing owls, the western prairie fringed orchid, and the prairie shooting star—have fallen victim to extensive habitat loss.

Clouds break over Corundum Point on Lake Superior.

Bald eagles and white pines are among Minnesota's premiere natural resources. (Photograph © Bill Marchel)

The list of life forms on the margins of survival runs long, but the news isn't necessarily all bad. The state's biological survey program has cataloged a comprehensive list of plant and animal species found in the wild. For most, the future is relatively secure. Some populations are in better shape now than they were twenty years ago. This improved status is particularly true for animals biologists characterize as "charismatic" species—the ones most likely to attract the public's interest. The gray wolf, for example, had dwindled to just a few hundred animals in northern Minnesota in the 1970s. Following a well-publicized recovery, the wolf now occupies suitable habitat as far south as the northern fringe of the Twin Cities' metropolitan area. Another success story is the bald eagle, one of several bird species devastated by DDT in the 1960s. The Environmental Protection Agency banned the pesticide, and birders once again spot eagles along our lakes and rivers. Sometimes, the wild even returns to a very civilized setting. Urban dwellers are occasionally startled to see a speedy, midsized bird chasing after city pigeons. Peregrine falcons are still very uncommon in Minnesota—just a few dozen live in the state—but a handful of the fast-flying raptors nest in the tall buildings of Minneapolis and St. Paul.

A skyscraper hardly constitutes natural habitat, but if a creature as wild as a peregrine falcon can survive in the midst of our populous metropolitan area, then there is hope for all things not tame. Our conservation efforts rest upon a sturdy foundation of natural resources. Minnesota contains far more public lands than any other state east of the Mississippi—and more than many western states, too. Dozens of state parks and natural areas protect ecosystems representative of our statewide biodiversity. Expansive forests and about one million acres of prairie wildlife areas provide a secure habitat base for common and not-so-common plants and animals. Healthy, self-sustaining fish populations thrive in our lakes and streams.

However, conservation's greatest resource comes from people. Minnesotans from all walks of life participate in conservation activities. Some teach kids about the outdoors. Others roll up their sleeves and volunteer for hard work on habitat-improvement projects. A few step up and speak for the wild at public meetings and political gatherings. Many Minnesotans belong to one or more nonprofit organizations, ranging from the Audubon Society to the Minnesota Deer Hunters Association.

Unfortunately, for every Minnesotan committed to conservation, dozens more are not. The state's population grew by about one million people in the last twenty years and is expected to gain another one million in the next twenty. The new residents will need homes, jobs, highways, and shopping malls. The greatest threat to our wild heritage is a slow death by a thousand cuts, a gradual attrition of natural habitat to accommodate growing numbers of people. Already, urban sprawl has crept north and west from the Twin Cities to St. Cloud. Suburbs that once functioned as distant bedroom communities for downtown workers now have become commuter destinations for workers living even farther from the urban core. On weekends, lines of traffic stream from the city, as urban dwellers seek fresh air and the freedom of open spaces. Unfortunately, they may be loving to death the woods and waters they so treasure. Rural real estate prices have skyrocketed as the affluent gobble up lakeshore lots, former farms, and forest parcels to build second homes. The tragic irony is that the desire to get closer to nature destroys what is sought, even though few may know it is gone. Once the new homes are built on the "Wolf Mountain" subdivision, the wolf pack doesn't come back to the ridge where they once rallied to howl beneath the moon.

In a society where most people live apart from nature and private-property rights are paramount, we will likely never stop sprawl. About the best we can hope for is to protect some places where eagles nest, fish spawn, and wolves howl. Our wealth of public land ensures that Minnesota remains truly wild. The wild we hold in common—the grandeur of a canoe-country sunset, the raucous arrival of migrating geese to Lac qui Parle, a sparkling trout stream in the Whitewater valley—are treasures of immeasurable value. We must pass this treasure on intact, even better that we found it, to coming generations.

Morning fog shrouds the St. Croix National Scenic River.

Right
Flying Canada geese are a timeless symbol of conservation.
(Photograph © Bill Marchel)

Below
A wisp of ground fog dawdles as dawn brightens an oak
savannah in central Minnesota.

A thunderstorm blows over the southwestern prairie and Blue Mounds State Park.

Icicles dangle over a dawn-colored Lake Superior.

CONSERVATION ORGANIZATIONS

The Audubon Society,
Minnesota State Office
2357 Ventura Drive, Suite 106
St. Paul, MN 55125
(651) 739-9332
mnaudubon@audubon.org

Friends of the Boundary
Waters Wilderness
401 North Third Street, Suite 290
Minneapolis, MN 55401-1475
(612) 332-9630
www.friends-bwca.org

Izaak Walton League of America,
Minnesota Division
555 Park Street, Suite 140
St. Paul, MN 55103
(651) 221-0215
(651) 649-1446
www.minnesotaikes.org

Land Stewardship Project
2200 4th Street
White Bear Lake, MN 55110
(651) 653-0618
www.landstewardshipproject.org

Minnesota Center for
Environmental Advocacy
26 East Exchange Street, Suite 206
St. Paul, MN 55101
(651) 223 5969
www.mncenter.org

Minnesota Deer Hunters Association
460 Peterson Road
Grand Rapids, MN 55744
(800) 450-3337
www.mndeerhunters.com

Minnesota Department
of Natural Resources
500 Lafayette Road
St. Paul, Minnesota 55155
(888) MINN DNR
www.dnr.state.mn.us

Minnesota Forestry Association
P.O. Box 496
Grand Rapids, MN 55744
(800) 821-8733
www.mnforest.com

Minnesota Forest Resources Council
2003 Upper Buford Circle
St. Paul, MN 55108-6146
www.frc.state.mn.us

Minnesota Ornithologists' Union
Bell Museum of Natural History
University of Minnesota
10 Church Street SE
Minneapolis, MN 55455-0104
(763) 780-8890
www.moumn.org

Minnesota Sea Grant
2305 East Fifth Street
208 Washburn Hall
Duluth, MN 55812
(218) 726-8106
www.seagrant.umn.edu

Minnesota Waterfowl Association
3750 Annapolis Lane, Suite 135
Plymouth, MN 55447
(763) 553-2977
www.mnwaterfowlassociation.org

Parks & Trails Council of Minnesota
275 East 4th Street #642
St. Paul, MN 55101
(651) 726-2457
www.parksandtrails.org

Pheasants Forever
1783 Buerkle Circle
St. Paul, MN 55110
(651) 773-2000
www.pheasantsforever.org.

The Nature Conservancy
of Minnesota
1101 West River Parkway, Suite 200
Minneapolis, MN 55415-1291
(612) 331-0750
minnesota@tnc.org

INDEX

Agassiz National Wildlife Refuge, 12, 20, 70, 148

Albert Lea Lake, 85

American Indians, *see* Lakota, Ojibwe, pictographs, petroglyphs, Pukaskwa Pits, Upper Sioux Indian Agency, U.S–Dakota Conflict of 1862

Arrowhead, 18, 51, 137, 147

Ashby, 73

aspen, 20, 21, 23, 29, 33, 91, 110, 119, 128, 130, 132, 145

bald eagle, 26, 28, 38, 152

Banning State Park, 12, 25

Baptism River, 12, 51, 61

Basswood Lake, 88

Basswood River, 103

Bean Lake, 83

Bear Head Lake State Park, 101

Bear Island State Forest, 69, 88, 97, 101

Bemidji, 20

Big Stone Lake, 29, 149

Big Stone National Wildlife Refuge, 29

Big Woods, 23, 128

birch, 20, 23, 33, 91, 94, 128, 130

Birch Lake, 69, 97

bird-watching, 109

Blackhoof River State Wildlife Management Area, 131

Blue Mounds State Park, 112, 115, 118, 155

blueberries, 87, 93–94

Bluestem Prairie, 108, 109, 123

Bonanza Prairie, 149

boreal owl, 52, 55

Boulder Lake, 139

Boundary Waters Canoe Area Wilderness, 20, 23, 52, 87, 88–105, 132, 148, 150

Bowstring Lake, 20

Brainerd, 12, 20, 130

Brule Lake, 92

buckthorn, 151

butterflies, 112, 123

Canada geese, 30, 41, 154

Canada lynx, 91, 101

Canadian Shield, 18

Cannon River, 26

Caribou Lake, 147

Carlos Avery State Wildlife Management Area, 70

carp, 31, 73–74, 151

Carter, Jimmy, 88

Cascade River, 33, 142

Cass Lake, 20

Chengwatana State Forest, 29, 143

Chippewa National Forest, 77, 81, 84, 128, 148

Civilian Conservation Corps, 26

Clean Water Act, 149

Cloquet State Forest, 139

commercial fishery, 49, 51

conservation, 23, 49, 51, 108, 148–153

Corundum Point, 151

cougars, 30

Crookston, 148

Crow Wing State Park, 12

Dalles of the St. Croix, 29, 41, 44

Dead Horse Lake, 81

Dorer, Richard, 128

Dragon's Tooth Rapids, 25

Driftless Area, 18

Duluth, 35, 52, 78, 130

Duluth Harbor, 151

Eagle Mountain, 18

early successional species, 94, 129
   see also blueberries, aspen, birch, jack pine

earthworms, 151

East Bay, 48

Eastern Tall Grass Prairie, 110

Echo Lake, 69

Ely, 88, 94

Environmental Protection Agency, 152

erosion, 20, 26, 27–28, 31, 128

Eurasian water milfoil, 151

Father Hennepin State Park, 72

Fenske Lake, 12

Finland, 52

fire, 94, 110, 112, 128

flooding, 27, 31, 149

Fond du Lac, 130

Ford Dam, 31

forestry, 23, 128, 129–130

Fort Charlotte, 18

Fort Ridgely State Park, 31, 121

Fort Snelling State Park, 32

Fur Trade, 18, 88

Glacial Lakes State Park, 124

Glacial Ridge National Wildlife Refuge, 148

glaciation, 18

Gooseberry River, 51, 55

Grand Marais, 48, 49, 55, 67

Grand Portage, 18, 51, 95

Grand Portage State Park, 25

Grand Rapids, 20, 130

Grassy Bay, 99

gray wolves, 29, 52, 55, 88, 91–92, 95, 152

great grey owl, 55, 64

Great Lakes, 18, 49, 151

Gulf of Mexico, 18, 20, 31, 75, 149

Gunflint Lake, 88

Gunflint Trail, 52, 94

Hastings, 29

Hat Point, 51, 55

Hawk Ridge, 52, 61

Heritage Hjemkomst Interpretative Center, 77

Hill City, 130

Hjemkomst, 77

Houston County, 26

Hudson Bay, 18, 20

Interstate State Park, 29

invasive species, *see* buckthorn, carp, earthworms, Eurasian water milfoil, purple loosestrife, rainbow smelt, round gobies, sea lampreys, zebra mussels

Itasca State Park, 20, 23, 26, 130, 131, 132

Itasca Wilderness Sanctuary, 132

jack pine, 94, 128–129, 130

Jack the Horse Lake, 84

Jay Cooke State Park, 12, 17, 36–37, 130

Jeffers Petroglyphs Historic Site, 112, 115

Kabetogama Lake, 20, 94, 150

Kettle River, 25, 29, 30, 130

Lac La Croix, 88, 95

Lac qui Parle, 80

Lac qui Parle Wildlife Management Area, 29

Lake Agassiz, 18, 20, 108

Lake Aitkin, 18

Lake Bronson State Park, 110, 119

Lake Christina, 73

Lake Duluth, 18

Lake Grantsburg, 18

Lake Itasca, 26, 151

Lake Lida, 77

Lake Minnesota, 18

Lake Minnetonka, 151

Lake of the Woods, 72, 73, 74, 75, 95

Lake Pepin, 33, 151

Lake Superior, 12, 18, 29, 36, 47–67, 95, 140, 150, 151, 156

Lake Traverse, 20

Lake Upham, 18

Lake Vermilion, 70

Lake Winnibigoshish, 20, 72

Lake Winnipeg, 20

Lakota, 31

Leaf Hills, 116
Leech Lake, 20, 70
Lincoln, Abraham, 31
Little Falls, 26
Little Long Lake, 77
loons, 17, 75, 83
Loon Lake, 73
Lost Forty, 128
Lower Basswood Falls, 103
Lower Red Lake, 20, 72
Lutsen, 18, 52
Manitoba, 30
Mankato, 18, 39
Marcy-Holmes Community Garden, 111
Marine on St. Croix, 44
mayflies, 92–93
McGregor, 35
migratory birds, 26, 30, 52, 55, 73, 75, 109
Mille Lacs Kathio State Park, 142
Mille Lacs Lake, 12, 70, 72
Minneapolis, 26, 152
Minneopa Creek, 39
Minneopa State Park, 39
Minnesota Department of Natural Resources,
    23
Minnesota Department of Public Health, 150
Minnesota Pollution Control Agency, 149
Minnesota River, 18, 29–31, 32, 34, 80, 109
Minnesota Valley National Fish and Wildlife
    Refuge, 32, 34
Mississippi River, 12, 18, 20, 22, 26–27,
    29, 31, 32, 38, 72, 109, 111, 130, 149,
    150–151
Moorhead, 77, 108
moose, 52, 91–92, 94, 95, 130
Moose Lake State Park, 69
muskellunge, 72–73
mussels, 31–32
Namakan Lake, 20, 94
Nature Conservancy, 108, 123, 148
New Ulm, 32
North Shore, 18–20, 47–67, 130, 131, 145,
    150
North Shore Drive, 48
North West Company Fur Post, 134
northern pike, 31, 72
oak savannahs, 21, 110, 128, 138, 154
Ojibway Lake, 94
Ojibwe, 70, 88–89, 95
old-growth forest, 129
paddlefish, 31
Palisade Head, 51, 62

peregrine falcons, 152
petroglyphs, 112, 115
pictographs, 88–89
Pigeon Point, 51
Pigeon River, 18, 25, 51
pileated woodpecker, 127
Pine City, 134
Pipestone Creek, 107
Pipestone National Monument, 107, 112
prairie chickens, 108, 110, 115
Preachers Grove, 20
Pukaskwa Pits, 52
purple loosestrife, 151
Quetico Provincial Park, 88
rainbow smelt, 49
Rainy Lake, 20, 94
Rainy River, 18, 148
Red Lake, 70
Red River of the North, 18, 20, 109
Rice Lake National Wildlife Refuge, 80
Richard Dorer Memorial Hardwood Forest,
    23
Ringo Lake, 12
River Warren, 18
Rochester, 30
Root River, 20, 22, 26
round gobies, 151
ruffed grouse, 55, 91, 130, 132, 137
Saganaga Lake, 88
Sakatah Lake, 79
Sand Point Lake, 94, 97, 98–99
Sandstone, 130
Savanna Portage State Park, 73, 147
Sawbill Trail, 52
Sawtooth Mountain Range, 18, 20, 54, 83,
    140, 147
Scott Lake, 21
sea lampreys, 49, 51
Seagull Lake, 87
Sherburne National Wildlife Refuge, 111, 117
Silver Bay, 64
Sioux quartzite, 107, 115, 118
snowshoe hare, 91, 130
Solana State Forest, 12
South Fowl Lake, 89
South Hegman Lake, 93
Spirit-Little-Cedar Tree, see Witch Tree
Split Rock Lighthouse, 59
spruce grouse, 55
St. Anthony Falls, 26
St. Cloud, 26
St. Croix State Forest, 29

St. Croix Wild and Scenic Riverway, 18,
    28–29, 31, 41, 42, 44, 130, 134, 153
St. Croix Wild River State Park, 29
St. Lawrence Seaway, 49
St. Louis River, 12, 17, 36–37, 38, 130
St. Mary's River, 48, 51
St. Paul, 26, 32, 152
St. Peter, 31
Stillwater, 29
sturgeon, 29, 31
Superior Hiking Trail, 18, 52, 140
Superior National Forest, 12, 18, 87, 94, 127,
    128
Susie Islands, 51
Tamarac National Wildlife Refuge, 20, 135
Taylors Falls, 29, 41
Temperance River, 12
Tettegouche State Park, 12, 61, 83, 145
Thief River Falls, 109
Thomson Reservoir, 78
Tofte, 52
turkeys, wild, 28, 29, 30, 130
Turtle Island, 104
Twain, Mark, 26
U.S.D.A. Forest Service, 88
U.S.–Dakota Conflict of 1862, 41
Upper Mississippi National Wildlife Refuge,
    27
Upper Red Lake, 20, 72
Upper Sioux Indian Agency, 41
Vermilion Lake, 104
Voyageurs Highway, 95, 150
Voyageurs National Park, 20–21, 23, 94–95,
    97
Wabasha, 26
Walker, 20
walleye, 29, 72–73, 90, 92, 150
West Savanna River, 35
wetlands, 148–149
white-tailed deer, 28, 29, 30, 32, 52, 64,
    91–92, 109, 119, 129, 137
Whitewater River, 26
Wild River State Park, 43, 142
William O'Brien State Park, 29
Winona, 32
Witch Tree, 51, 55
Wolf Creek, 28
Yellow Medicine Indian Agency, see Upper
    Sioux Indian Agency
zebra mussels, 32, 151
Zumbro River, 20, 26

ABOUT THE AUTHOR
AND PHOTOGRAPHER

Photograph © Scott Benson

Photograph © Carmelita Nelson

SHAWN PERICH LIVES in Hovland, Minnesota, on Lake Superior's North Shore. His writings on conservation and the outdoors appear in numerous publications, including a long-running column in *Minnesota Outdoor News*. The author of several books, including *Backroads of Minnesota* (2002), he is also the publisher of *Northern Wilds*, a quarterly publication devoted to outdoor activities in the north country. When he isn't writing, Perich enjoys trout fishing and roaming the north woods with his dogs.

UTILIZING A LARGE-FORMAT 4x5 field camera, native Minnesotan Gary Alan Nelson photographs wild places and rural landscapes throughout North America. His images have been published by the Audubon Society, *Backpacker Magazine*, *Men's Journal*, various *National Geographic* publications, *National Wildlife*, the National Parks Conservation Association, The Nature Conservancy, *Outdoor Photographer*, *Outside*, the Sierra Club, and the Wilderness Society. Photographs in this book are available as fine art prints at www.garyalannelson.com.